EVANGELICALS AND DEVELOPMENT

CONTEMPORARY ISSUES IN SOCIAL ETHICS
Ronald J. Sider, General Editor

Lifestyle in the Eighties: An Evangelical Commitment
  to Simple Lifestyle, *ed. Ronald J. Sider*
Evangelicals and Development: Toward a Theology
  of Social Change, *ed. Ronald J. Sider*

General Preface

An historic transformation is in process. In all parts of the world, evangelical Christians in growing numbers are rediscovering the biblical summons to serve the poor, minister to the needy, correct injustice and seek societal shalom. The Chicago Declaration of Evangelical Social Concern (1973), the Lausanne Covenant's section on social responsibility (1974), the Evangelical Fellowship of India's Madras Declaration on Evangelical Social Action (1979) and the Evangelical Commitment to Simple Lifestyle (1980) are symptomatic of far-reaching change. A fundamentally new worldwide movement is emerging. It seeks justice and peace in the power of the Spirit. It consists of biblical Christians passionately committed to a new search for social justice that is thoroughly biblical, deeply immersed in prayer, and totally dependent on the presence of the Holy Spirit.

Substantive theological and ethical reflection is imperative if the growing movement of evangelical social concern is to be biblical and effective. The Unit on Ethics and Society of the Theological Commission of the World Evangelical Fellowship hopes this new series of books, *Contemporary Issues in Social Ethics*, will contribute to that goal. We hope and believe that evangelicals will have something significant and different to add to current debates on urgent social questions. But we dare never forget that other Christians have long been discussing these problems. Hoping to avoid reinventing the wheel, we intend to profit from what others have written and done. We also acknowledge in painful repentance that we have too long neglected what we ought to have done.

The Unit on Ethics and Society of the World Evangelical Fellowship believes that the content of the volumes in the forthcoming series merits the careful attention of all Christians although the Unit does not necessarily endorse every viewpoint expressed.

Ronald J. Sider,
Convener
Unit on Ethics & Society
Theological Commission
World Evangelical Fellowship

EVANGELICALS AND DEVELOPMENT
Toward a Theology of Social Change

Edited by
RONALD J. SIDER

THE WESTMINSTER PRESS
Philadelphia

Copyright © World Evangelical Fellowship 1981

Published by The Westminster Press
Philadelphia, Pennsylvania

PRINTED IN THE UNITED STATES OF AMERICA
9 8 7 6 5 4 3 2 1

Library of Congress Cataloging in Publication Data

Main entry under title:

Evangelicals and development.

(Contemporary issues in social ethics ; v. 2)
Papers from the Consultation on the Theology of
Development held Mar. 10-14, 1980, High Leigh Conference
Centre, Hoddesdon, England, sponsored by the Unit on
Ethics and Society of the Theological Commission of the
World Evangelical Fellowship.
Includes index.
1. Church and underdeveloped areas—Congresses.
2. Evangelicalism—Congresses. I. Sider, Ronald J.
II. Consultation on the Theology of Development (1980 :
High Leigh Conference Centre) III. World Evangelical
Fellowship. Unit on Ethics and Society. IV. Series.
BR115.U6E88   1982   261.8   82-6970
ISBN 0-664-24445-9   AACR2

Contents

64805

Introduction

RONALD J. SIDER

The explosive growth of evangelical development agencies represents one of the more significant areas of change in evangelical circles in the last few decades. Three decades ago, relief and development was a peripheral concern for evangelicals. Today evangelical relief and development agencies raise and distribute hundreds of millions of dollars each year.

This development reflects a growing reappropriation of the biblical concern for the poor, hungry and oppressed. It also reflects countless sacrificial decisions by unknown people who decided to give $5, $50 or $200 for famine relief in the Sahel or long-range development in India rather than spend it on themselves. One can only thank God.

This awakening evangelical concern for the poor comes at a desperate period in global history. In 1980, both the Brandt Commission on International Development and *The Global 2000 Report to the President* (U.S.) indicated that the growing gap between rich and poor poses a dangerous threat to world peace. "If mankind is to survive, says Brandt and his colleagues, the gap between the rich and the poor must be closed — quickly."[1] *Global Report 2000* paints a foreboding picture of the year 2000:

If present trends continue, the world in 2000 will be more crowded, more polluted, less stable ecologically, and more vulnerable to disruption than the world we live in now . . . For hundreds of millions of the desperately poor, the outlook for food and other necessities of life will be no better. For many it will be worse . . . . The large existing gap between the rich and poor nations widens.[2]

Reshaping the relationships between the poor in the Southern hemisphere and the well-off in the Northern hemisphere is, according to the Brandt Commission, "the greatest challenge to mankind for the remainder of this century."[3]

The enormous growth of evangelical relief and development activities demonstrates a strong desire to rise to this challenge. Problems, however, have arisen as programmes have increased rapidly. How can money and resources be shared in a way that involves genuine partnership rather than paternalism? In what way should development activities be related to local churches? What is the relationship of development to the total mission of the church, especially evangelism? To what extent should development agencies deal with questions of injustice where unjust social structures create poverty and/or prevent change? What can evangelicals learn from the vast volume of literature on development written by others (both secular and religious) in the last couple of decades?

Persistent questions such as these prompted the Unit on Ethics and Society of the Theological Commission of the World Evangelical Fellowship to sponsor a five-day "Consultation on the Theology of Development".[4] Invitations were sent to a wide range of evangelicals involved with development: most Western relief and development agencies; Third World development agencies; development specialists; church leaders and theologians from all continents. From March 10-14, 1980, 41 persons from about 17 different countries (see the names in the Appendix) assembled at the High Leigh Conference Centre, Hoddesdon, England for the Consultation. Financial assistance was generously given by Christoffelblindenmission, Compassion, Mennonite Central Committee, Tear Fund (UK), World Concern, World Vision (Australia) and World Vision International.

The consultation began with prepared papers. Vinay Samuel and Chris Sugden ably surveyed the literature on the theology of development (see Chapter 2) and then offered their own suggestions for a theology of development and social change (see Chapter 3). Tom Sine shared his expertize as an historian and futurologist in his paper on development's secular past and uncertain future (Chapter 4). As director of a large Third World development agency (EFICOR), Col. M. R. Mathews probed the implications of Western theologies of development for Third World countries and churches (Chapter 5).

The papers stirred vigorous, creative debate. Especially significant was the strong insistence of Third World leadership that the question of social structures which create poverty must receive new attention. That concern receives articulate expression in the "Statement of Intent" (see Chapter 1) issued by the consultation.

The participants decided that a three-year programme (Christian Involvement in Human Development: A Programme of Evangelical Study and Action) was needed, and a Steering Committee was appointed.[5] Meeting on January 31 to February 1, 1981, the Steering Committee defined the goals and mapped out an ambitious three-year programme.

Goal I: "We seek to promote theological reflection on attempts to meet human need in concrete local development situations." Persons involved in concrete development work (in both local, Third World development projects and international and national agency offices) will be invited to write up, analyze, and reflect theologically on case studies of development work. Of special concern in the process will be the attempt to ask how biblical norms and perspectives do and/or ought to shape the concrete character of development work. What are relevant biblical criteria for evaluating development work? How should a concern for evangelism, justice, Christian community, servanthood, redistribution of power, partnership, etc., be integrated into goal-setting and evaluation? A large number of case studies will be collected and brought to a Stage I Consultation in June, 1982. Additional groups will be invited to collect additional case studies in preparation for Consultation '83, a major international consultation on evangelical development work.

Goal II: "We seek further clarification of theological issues related to development." Vigorous disagreement exists over the relationship of development to the total mission of the church. To what extent is it legitimate biblically to engage in development without attention to questions of both evangelism and social justice? Six theological papers will be prepared,[6] analyzed by the local groups preparing case studies, and presented at the Stage I Consultation in 1982. After revision, further analysis by additional local groups and regional consultations, they will be presented at Consultation '83, revised once more and then published as a monograph.

In addition to the activities designed to implement the above goals, the three-year programme will seek to develop new models for theological reflection on development and promote the dissemination of development curricula for theological schools. We hope and pray that the Lord of the church will direct and guide these various programmes in order to improve and strengthen evangelical involvement in development.

It is hoped that the publication of this volume of material from the initial consultation will stimulate further discussion and contribute to the on-going activity of tens of thousands of

persons around the world working to reduce poverty, suffering
and injustice. It is by no means a final statement. It presents
ideas to be examined and tested. The authors speak for themselves. They do not speak for the World Evangelical Fellowship's Theological Commission whose Unit on Ethics and Society
sponsored the High Leigh Consultation.

All income from this book will go to the continuing programme of the Unit on Ethics and Society.

Ronald J. Sider, Convener
Unit on Ethics & Society
Theological Commission
World Evangelical Fellowship

CHAPTER ONE
A Statement of Intent

1

A Statement of Intent

(This statement was issued by the Consultation on the Theology of Development, March 10-14, 1980, High Leigh Conference Centre, Hoddesdon, England. For the list of participants, see the Appendix.)

As we stand at the threshold of the 1980s we are deeply disturbed by much of what we see in the contemporary world.

We are deeply disturbed by the human suffering present in the agonizing realities of hunger, malnutrition, disease, unemployment, illiteracy, deprivation and starvation.

We are deeply disturbed by the inability or unwillingness of the governments of the world to grapple with this injustice and tragedy.

We are deeply disturbed by the rising occurrence of violence and conflict within many of our societies and between many of them. The growth in the international arms trade gives particular cause for acute concern.

We are deeply disturbed that the difference in standards of living between the rich and the poor continues to increase.

We are deeply disturbed by many activities undertaken in the name of development which are leading to further injustices and suffering.

We are deeply disturbed that many of the social, economic and political structures of our societies are pervaded by injustice and violence.

We are deeply disturbed by the gross violation of human rights that continues to be committed in many of our societies.

We are deeply disturbed by the extent of apathy within the Christian church in the face of widespread suffering and injustice in the world.

We recognize that the Bible teaches that the mission of the church includes the proclamation of the gospel and the demonstration of its relevance by working for community development and social change.

We recognize that the church is called to work for that justice in society which God wills and to help people to enjoy the fullness of life which is God's purpose for all people.

We recognize that in order to engage in social change and model the relationships it commends for society, the church must exhibit total dependence on the transforming power of the Holy Spirit of God.

In the light of this understanding of scripture we resolve with God's help to live out the full Christian gospel and to apply it to the needy situations in which we find ourselves.

We resolve, in the company of others within the church, to study more deeply the current social, political and economic issues, which are so heavily influencing the lives of the world's population.

We resolve to change many of the attitudes that we find within ourselves which contribute to poverty and injustice.

We resolve to place greater trust in God and greater trust in each other in order to build relationships which will encourage and strengthen us in our common task to relieve poverty and injustice.

We resolve to encourage, by all the peaceful and constructive means available to us, the poor and oppressed who are seeking to establish a position of dignity and self-worth.

Finally we resolve to reconsider the use of the resources which God has given us, in order that such resources may contribute more effectively to God's kingdom and righteousness, love and justice.

CHAPTER TWO

Theology of Development: A Guide to the Debate

Theology of Development: A Guide to the Debate

VINAY SAMUEL and CHRIS SUGDEN

Introduction

What is development? Development is a *process*. "Development is a process by which people gain greater control over themselves, their environment and their future, in order to realize the full potential of life that God has made possible."[1] Development is a process towards a goal.

What is theology of development? Theology of development is *reflection* on the reasons for Christian involvement in development, the method of involvement, and the goal of involvement from a Christian and biblical perspective.

The nature of involvement in development by the church and by Christian agencies is clearly affected by the *motivation* for involvement. Motivation is based both on a group's *world view* and their *theology*. It is based on their view of God's purpose: what is the full potential of life that God has made possible? It is based on their view of God's activity: how does he achieve this goal? It is based on their view of God's people: what is their role in God's activity? As we survey the literature on theology of development we will see that the way people answer these three questions is related to their theology *and* their world view.

Bases for Christian Involvement in Development

All Christians agree that Christian involvement in development flows out of Christ's command to love our neighbour. In loving our neighbour we are linking ourselves with God's own work in human society. On this there is agreement. Debate arises when we try and understand how God works in society. We identify two major understandings of how God works in society that inform current Christian involvement in development.

(i) *God's work in providence.* God's concern runs throughout the whole of his creation, to sustain and preserve human life. Development is the activity of the church to put this concern into practice. The church fulfills God's intention to preserve human life.

(ii) *The activity of God in Christ.* God's activity in the world is more than a providential intention to sustain human life. God is at work in all human history within and beyond the church to apply the redemption summed up in Christ. The whole process of God's work in creation, judgment and redemption is seen and achieved in the person and work of his Son, Jesus Christ. God is at work to apply the results of the atonement and resurrection to the whole of creation. The role of the church is to co-operate with God's dynamic activity and be instruments of his work.

Historical Survey

As we briefly survey the church's thinking on developing human life, we will see this interaction between world view and theology.

From the first to the seventeenth centuries the motivation for the church's involvement with social change in relation to the poor was personal charity.[2] Its architect was Augustine and his doctrine of charity: obey God in order to win salvation. The world and its social order was relativized by the priority of love for God. Social change was of secondary importance to the priority of loving God. Care for the poor was therefore essentially a means to win salvation. "While this was a stimulus to insightful and human actions and laws, its superstructure rendered it incapable of formulating social policies to deal with major economic and social change."[3] The world view of the medieval church was to maintain the status quo, and this was determined by its theology.

With the Reformation came a fundamental theological shift in the understanding of the church's involvement in society, especially in relation to poverty and the poor.

Luther's theological position consists essentially of the conviction that salvation is not the process or goal of life, but rather its presupposition . . . Since righteousness before God is by faith alone and salvation is the source rather than the goal of life, it becomes difficult to rationalize the plight of the poor as a peculiar form of blessedness. There is no salvific value in being poor or in giving alms. Thus when the Reformers turned to the reform of poor relief and social policy, they had a new theological foundation for their work . . . They de-ideologized the medieval approach to the poor which had obscured the problem of poverty.[4]

Luther and his colleague Karlstadt made provision in Wittenberg for the city council to provide low-interest loans for workers; subsidies for education and training for the children of the poor; taxes to support the poor — all designed to *prevent* as well as alleviate poverty. In five years they changed the theory and practice of poor relief which had been established by centuries of ecclesiastical tradition. They were convinced that fundamental human rights of equality, freedom and brotherly love had their source in the Christian faith. This task of social change was essentially a task for the secular ruler and kingdom to carry out. This was the birth of the two kingdoms theory, which is the basis of motivation two.

The next period, which is the birth of the modern era, saw the simultaneous expansion of the western nations in colonialism, and the beginning of the world-wide expansion of the church through the modern western Protestant missionary movement. The church's involvement in society was primarily the establishment of churches in 'pagan lands'. The theological basis for this involvement in society was again the two kingdoms theology of Luther. Social change was left to the secular ruler. Any provision of social care such as education was for the furtherance of the gospel, so that people could read the scriptures and teach the church.

The contemporary scene reveals a major shift which has taken place primarily in the churches in the newly independent and third world countries. The stark reality of poverty and revolutions for sudden social change have forced themselves as major items on to the church's agenda. The major focus of the church's reflection has been to define the activity of God in relation to these realities and thus to clarify its role in relation to his activity. This shift is not yet paralleled by a similar shift in the reflection of the western church, where neither poverty nor social change by revolutionary means are part of national life. Therefore a tension has arisen between western and third world churches in co-operative efforts for mission and development. This has led some church leaders in the Third World to call for a complete moratorium on western involvement, and for some mission strategists in the western world to call for a new expansion of mission which is forced to bypass the national church.[5] It is therefore imperative that we survey and evaluate strategies for the church's involvement in society by both third world and western churches from a biblical perspective. At the centre of these strategies is a vision of what society ought to be, and where God is at work in the world — in other words, a world view and a theology.

We identify the theological questions as follows:

What is a Christian view of how society ought to be?
What are the sociological and political reasons why it is not like this?
What are the means by which the present situation of society should be changed to conform to the Christian vision?
How far do our own values and assumptions about society conform to Christian criteria?

These questions focus on the central issues of where, how and to what end is God at work in the world? The answer to this question depends on what view of the kingdom of God and of the nature of evil we take. We will survey the answers which theologians give to these questions in a continent-by-continent presentation. We will see how theologians' answers are related to their context. In general terms we can locate their answers to the question "How does God work in the world?" on a spectrum from violent revolution through liberation and humanization to modernization.

Latin America — God works through Liberation

We will begin at a position left of centre of the spectrum with Latin American theologians of liberation, because in many ways they sparked off new theological debate in this whole area.[6]

What is their context? Their countries are nominally Christianized — the legacy of Spanish and Portuguese imperialism. They are nominally independent politically, as colonial rule ended in the last century. And they are poor. Measured by per capita GNP they are not so poor as many countries in South Asia or Africa, but by western standards they are poor. Large numbers of the population live in appalling conditions.

In this context a number of theologians began to ask why such poverty existed, what God was doing about it and what the church should do about it. They rejected western theological categories for answering these questions for two reasons. First they felt that western theological categories asked the question "Does God exist in a scientific world and how can an individual know him?" Their question was a different one: "What will

God do for a poor man and a poor community?'' Secondly western theological categories basically assumed that an evolutionary process to improve liberal democratic structures would
bring a measurable social improvement.

The theologians of liberation were convinced that gradual
change was not the answer. They claimed to find a more adequate explanation for what they saw as the economic colonization of their countries in the Marxist categories of the division
of society into oppressor and oppressed groups.

Development in this context cannot come through economic
growth because it is the economic system itself which is responsible for the poverty. More of the same will solve nothing. What
people need, to attain this goal of control of their own destiny
to fulfil their God-given potential, is liberation from the bondage of economic structures which prevent this. Anything else is
merely painting the prison walls. New structures are needed,
both within the country and internationally, because the oppressor groups maintain their position by alliance with international
structures of injustice (e.g. terms of trade, multinational com-
panies, capitalism).

Latin American liberation theology is essentially a reflection
on the content, meaning and means of Christian obedience
given the validity of the Marxist analysis, and given the gospel.
Latin American theologians ask what it means to be the church
in the circumstances of poverty and injustice. The use that
Roman Catholic theologians make of the Marxist analysis to
understand poverty and injustice could have the status of
natural revelation of the facts of the case. For Protestants the
analysis forms part of the context for the church's and the
Christian's obedience to the demands of the gospel. The Marxist analysis contributes to the description of how God acts to
bring his justice. He does not act only through the ballot box
and measured Parliamentary debate, he also acts through his
church engaging in changing current unjust structures. If we ask
whether there is any biblical precedent for God's acting in sudden change to alter unjust structures, liberation theologians
point to the Exodus, the message of the prophets interpreting
the judgment of Samaria and Jerusalem, and Jesus' prophecy of
the destruction of Jerusalem.

Both Roman Catholics and liberal and evangelical Protestants contribute to this understanding of God as one who acts
by setting people free from unjust structures. The Latin American Theological Fraternity is a fellowship of evangelical theologians who have entered into significant dialogue with the

writings of liberation theologians.[7] The members of the Fraternity offer us a biblical reflection on the theses of liberation theology, and also help us see important insights that this theology gives us into the biblical material. These reflections surfaced at the Lausanne Congress on World Evangelization (1974) where Rene Padilla and Samuel Escobar's papers not only contributed to the stress in the Lausanne Covenant that we should share "God's concern for justice and reconciliation throughout human society and for the liberation of men from every form of oppression," but also stimulated a statement on Radical Discipleship by a large minority of the Congress which reflected on the church's previous involvements in society:

We confess that: We have often been in bondage to a particular culture and sought to spread it in the name of Jesus.

We have not been aware of when we have debased and distorted the Gospel by a contrary value system.

We have been partisan in our condemnation of totalitarianism and violence, and have failed to condemn societal and institutionalized sin, especially that of racism.

We have sometimes so identified ourselves with particular political systems that the Gospel has been compromised and the prophetic voice muted.

We have frequently denied the rights and neglected the cries of the underprivileged and those struggling for freedom and justice.[8]

In reflecting on liberation theology, Padilla, Escobar and other evangelicals in the LATF pose the question: "Is the Marxist analysis or the Bible normative for discerning God's action?" They caution against a hasty answer. They agree with liberation theologians that it is not possible to participate in theological reflection from an ivory tower. Everyone has a perspective and commitment to a set of values which may or may not be biblical. This commitment is revealed more by what we do than by what we say. Padilla and Escobar however warn that we may take an evangelical stance that the Bible is normative but in fact base our actions in development on certain answers about God's action which are informed by our world view. If we read our answers into the Bible and identify them with 'what the Bible teaches', we allow our analysis of society to be normative for our own understanding of the Bible.

Therefore the members of the LATF agree with liberation theologians that theology is not only a reflection on God's action in a situation 'out there'. It is also a critical analysis of one's own biases and commitments by other criteria, and for the

LATF these are the biblical criteria of a society of justice and shalom. In dialogue with liberation theologians in Latin America, members of the LATF stress that in the Bible God's strategy for changing structures is essentially non-violence; it is not brought about through violent revolution. But they urge on their evangelical brethren in Europe and North America that in the Bible God's strategy may be more confrontational and conflictual than evangelicals have been accustomed to think. Both liberal theologians and evangelicals must examine their prior commitments about the nature of social change in the light of the Bible. The biblical goal of a just society can be achieved only through a biblical gospel and a biblical strategy. Members of the Fraternity therefore appreciate the insistence of liberation theologians that we examine our cultural commitments and the biases revealed in our actions. We can never be entirely free of them, but we should be conscious of them and evaluate them in the light of the scriptures.

Members of the Fraternity are also critically appreciative of the analysis of evil that liberation theology advances. In some ways, liberation theology is the social gospel of the earlier twentieth century without its evolutionary optimism. The goal of God's just society can be attained only through conflict with deep-seated evil in individuals and social structures. As evangelicals seek to develop biblical criteria for social change, members of the LATF urge us to see that attempts to improve society through education, grants and training may be counterproductive if we do not perceive that the social system itself, within which we educate people, may be the cause of injustice. If we neglect to see this, we will fall into the same mistake as the earlier proponents of the social gospel. The key question is "How can this structural evil be overcome?" If we engage in the traditional evangelical analysis that society is only the sum total of individuals, and that the way to change society is by changing individuals *alone*, the LATF asks us to go back to the earlier question whether this analysis of society and evil is biblical, or informed by individualistic western culture. They urge that serious biblical study shows that Moses, the prophets, Jesus and Paul diagnosed evil as personal, social and cosmic. For example, the Israelite monarchy and Jerusalem society became so unjust that God judged them and raised up new social structures among the people of Israel and in the Christian community. These new structures could come about only when evil on a cosmic scale was defeated, and the Lordship of Jesus Christ over the whole of life was established. This cosmic liberation from evil makes possible not only individual repentance, but the creation of a new community, the church, with structures which promise justice and shalom.[9]

Not all liberation theologians would agree with the LATF about the centrality of Jesus' cosmic act of liberation from evil. Some would concentrate more on the validity of revolution as the overthrow of structural evil. However, their questions about how structural evil may be removed have prompted the LATF to examine afresh the biblical data on Christ's death, resurrection and victory over evil.

In summary, for Latin American theologians of liberation, God acts to achieve a just society by changing structures (although not necessarily through violence). The church cannot undertake the development process without analyzing and changing social structures; she must educate her members to do this and produce in her own fellowship structures which model God's justice for society. This is the process of liberation.

A British evangelical, Michael Eastman, is secretary of the department of the Scripture Union which is concerned with mission among underprivileged youth. He writes the following positive appreciation and summary of liberation theology. His positive assessment is due in some part to the fact that he is grappling with similar issues among the deprived in inner cities in Britain. This would prompt us to examine the social position of those who dismiss liberation theology. Eastman writes,

All liberation theologians stress that life as it is lived and experienced, the things that happen in the actual world, is where God's mission is located and where theology begins.

We need to understand our historical reality and for this the tools of the human sciences, sociology, politics, economics, behavioural and cultural and historical studies, are indispensable. So too is an understanding of how the present actual historical situation can be changed, biblical reflection which in turn gives rise not only to ideas but also to strategies and tactics which can be applied. There is therefore a dynamic interaction (dialectic) between action and reflection. This real world is not static or closed or absolute. It is highly mobile, open and always provisional. Hence the importance of 'conscientization' — i.e. becoming alive to why things are as they are and how they can be changed.[10]

East Europe and Russia

Russia and Eastern Europe have experienced social change

inspired by adopting a Marxist understanding of social change as the overthrow of a dominant oppressive class by means of the oppressed people organizing themselves and using any means to achieve their end. Though the early days of the Russian Revolution placed great emphasis on people's participation through the soviets, the revolution came progressively to rely on direction from the party leadership imposed by force.

Governments in the Communist Countries of Europe seem to have little interest in development in the poor countries. Their aim is to bring political revolution in Third World countries for they hold that a communist style of government is the only means for bringing social change for the benefit of the poor. Political change will automatically result in development by a redistribution of resources and power. Their goal in developing countries is to follow the pattern of their own countries: redistribution of political power is primary and economic growth and personal freedom are secondary. Unless this order of priorities changes within the communist countries themselves, third world countries that accept the aid or the pattern of communist countries will find they will have to accept this sequence of events and priorities.

The churches in these countries seem to have little involvement in development in poorer countries, presumably because of their own beleaguered position and because of the limitations set by their context.

Theological reflection among western churches on the social change of the Russian Revolution was at first negative. The Russian revolution was violent, atheistic, totalitarian and therefore wrong. Pope Pius XI described Communism in 1937 as intrinsically perverting.[11]

Dialogue with Marxists in Europe began after the wind of change that blew through Communism after the end of the Stalinist era, and through the Roman Catholic Church at the succession of John XXIII. The background and issues are described by Andrew Kirk.[12] But such dialogue was not reflection on action, as was the dialogue in Latin America; it was dialogue on theory. The substance of the debate was principally two related issues. First, did religion advance or retard human progress? Secondly, could Marxism provide an adequate understanding of individual man without a concept of God? These questions reflect the essentially theoretical, scientific and existential bias of Europe. It was dialogue that neither arose from nor led to action. Poverty and social change to rectify injustice were not on the agenda.

Asia

What are the contours of Asia? It is a continent of religion. Ancient cultures and self-confident religions have resisted the mission of the church. It is a continent of poverty and plenty. The GNP of India is far below any in Latin America,[13] and yet Japan sports a modern economic miracle paralleled only by Western Germany. It is a continent of revolution. In China Communism not only ended one hundred years of Christian missionary expansion, but claimed to succeed in transforming Chinese society where Christian mission had failed. Other countries struggle to ensure the survival of their millions. Some, like India are torn between limiting certain human rights and political dissent in order to let the government impose the discipline necessary to make the economy work, and allowing freedom to organize opposition to government or management in order to allow maximum participation by all people in building their own lives. Other countries are torn between subservience to foreign powers which brings certain economic benefits and some repression at home, or complete political autonomy and a danger of anarchy and internal collapse.

Within this context the Christian church is both a minority and an alien community. Christian theological reflection on what God is doing in Asia centres on these contours.

Asian theological reflection calls first for an authentic Asian church. In many parts of Asia the church exists as an alien. Missionaries assumed that what they taught their converts was universally Christian, whereas it was also set in western forms. They assumed that there was a universally valid form of Christian worship, creed, lifestyle and theological reflection. They assumed that if they taught their converts to be authentically Christian, they would automatically become authentically Asian. China has rejected such a church. Elsewhere the Asian church is only a subsidiary of western mission boards which are suspicious of anything that appears to question western-formulated Christianity.

What will this authentic church look like? Choan-Seng Song of China argues that it will be discontinuous with the western understanding of the church as central to God's mission. He writes:

The colossal efforts of western churches for more than a century to incorporate the masses of humanity on the Asian continent into 'salvation history' faltered and were shaken to the roots (when China became a Communist state) . . . An understanding of Christian mission in terms of evangelizing and converting the pagans and bringing them into the fold of the church is irrelevant in the context of modern China. We are faced with the agonizing question: "What does it mean to speak of the 'hand of God' at work in China today?"[14]

Elsewhere he continues:

The chapter of missionary expansion in China was closed. Many Christians thought that was also the end of God's mission work in China. But this was too simplistic a conclusion, a conclusion based on unfaith and on the presumption that the mission of the church represented the whole of God's mission . . . There have been signs that the redemptive power of God's mission has not ceased to work in the people of China . . . The Church is not in control of the destiny of the world. The world's destiny is in God's hands.[15]

According to Song, Western theologians forced the history of God's redemption into the history of the Jews and the Christian church and insisted that all other redemption should be a linear development and expansion of this. But, Song says, Christians must know how other people see and experience redemption and hope, in the sufferings which descend on them from within the framework of their own history and tradition. Christian perspective must be discontinuous with the history of the Christian church, just as Jesus made a radical break with the expectations of the Jews and as Paul had to break with his Pharisaic background to carry the gospel of Christ to the Gentiles.[16]

Some Indian theologians reflect on the development of Indian society and, in similar fashion to Song, do not see the role of the church as central.[17] The church was allied with the British raj and, if anything, opposed the march for independence. However Christianity had a profound but unintentional effect on India's development. The movements for national independence and for development of every group in society did not arise within the church, but from the impact of Christianity on Hinduism. Hinduism covers the religion of the Aryan invaders who suppressed the lower groups. It is a religious culture of oppression.[18] Concepts of freedom and development, especially of the poorest, are not part of its heritage. The effect of Christianity was to humanize Hinduism. God is at work not just in the church, but in the interface, the dialogue, the meeting of Jesus Christ with other societies, religions and philosophies, making them more human. God's action is whatever makes for human values. His mission occurs in dialogue to affirm human values in other philosophies and religions.

According to these writers, development is humanization and

the role of the church is in keeping with its minority status; it is essentially peripheral. The work of groups concerned for justice and humanization has therefore taken place mainly outside the traditional structures of the church, and of theological education. Reflection has taken place among such groups as the Christian Institute for the Study of Religion and Society in Bangalore, the Delhi Christian Forum, and the Urban and Industrial Rural Mission. But such groups are informed by an ecclesiology that sees the church in larger terms than the body that consciously acknowledges Jesus as Lord. This could partly have arisen out of their impatience with the many contradictions they perceive within the body of Christ in India.

Evangelical writers on development in India cannot accept such an evaluation of the role of the church. But they agree that the questions are valid and demand relevant answers from the scriptures. Vinay Samuel and Chris Sugden point out that in Scripture the Lordship of God over history and over the nations is always focused on the deliverance of God's people; the justice which they establish in their society, to mirror his justice; their protection of the poorest and weakest; their right relationships of forgiveness and reconciliation; and their calling to warn of God's judgment on social and structural injustice.[19] The Lordship of God in Christ over the nations cannot be experienced or expressed without a community that acknowledges and demonstrates the results of obedience to Jesus as Lord.

Therefore, the church must analyze the social system in which it is set by biblical values. In India religion sanctions social status and economic power. Most attempts to protest against the dominance of the wealthy minority have been rejected or absorbed by the dominant group. Christian mission work in schools and hospital began by giving priority to the poorest groups. But they now benefit the élite, for when they were deprived of the imperial umbrella Christian institutions needed the money, favour and patronage of the wealthy élites to survive. In winning these, they can lose their freedom to challenge the injustice by which the wealthy élites maintain their position. They are absorbed into the caste system, to bolster the position of dominant élites. If Christian development concentrates on church growth or economic growth without perceiving that God would use the church to initiate social change, she becomes a captive of an oppressive culture.

In dialogue with those of other religions, the church will need to remember that the social structures and injustices of those religions often perpetuate injustice, inequality, and oppression of women. The church betrays its Lord by compromise on these matters also. Dialogue will not consist in mutual denunciation of false gods or the evaluation of the relative worth of truth in each religion. It will seek to discover where the Lord of history is at work, what his goal is, whom he is using as instruments and to what truths he is pointing. The prime witness in the Christian contribution will be the evidence of God's power working in her own community to bring justice, love and shalom. Therefore the church must constantly evaluate her own community life by the biblical criteria of a just human community. It must be ready to discern God at work bringing those features of a just human society through other instruments than the church, evaluate them and work alongside them to witness to the one whose very name is Shalom. A non-Christian Indian development leader watched Christian development groups and read his Bible for two years, for he is convinced that Jesus is the only motivation and inspiration for true development.

Vishal Mangalwadi asks the church to analyze carefully the economic realities of Indian society: "In India it is estimated that it costs the state over one lakh rupees (£6000) to make a child a doctor . . . This amount eventually comes from our primary producers in rural India. But how many doctors are there, even Christian doctors, who use this privilege either to amass wealth for themselves in western countries, or to further exploit the poor of India through the training they have received at the cost of poor people's labour?"[20]

Mangalwadi goes to the Scripture with this analysis and finds that Jesus commanded the rich young ruler to give his money back to the people from whom it had come to him through unjust means. He did not ask him to give his money for evangelism or to the temple. It had to be returned to its rightful owners, the poor. Such repentance means that western giving to India should be in a spirit of gratitude to those who have contributed to their affluence, and that Indian Christians should adopt similar lifestyles.

Africa

There are four theologies of development in Africa which we will locate at different points on the spectrum.

We first describe the approach of Julius Nyerere, which may be called participation.[21]

The context of Middle Africa is of countries which have recently emerged from colonial rule. Economic problems abound. Tanzania's GNP is 180 dollars per capita (India's is 150). But Nyerere sees that the road to development is for people to overcome the psychological and political shackles of colonialism, where everything was done to them and for them, not by them. He stresses the need to build a society whose political structures promote community, responsibility and participation. He writes:

People cannot be developed; they can only develop themselves. For, while it is possible for an outsider to build a man's house, an outsider cannot give the man pride and self-confidence in himself as a human being. Those things a man has to create in himself by his own actions. He develops himself by what he does; he develops himself by making his own decisions, by increasing his understanding of what he is doing, and why; by increasing his own knowledge and ability, and by his own full participation — as an equal — in the life of the community he lives in. Thus for example a man is developing himself if he grows or earns enough to provide decent conditions for himself and his family: he is not being developed if he is given these things.[22]

Nyerere's theological reflection is based on his view of man in society. He writes:

Man lives in society. He becomes meaningful to himself and his fellows only as a member of that society. Therefore to talk of the development of man and to work for the development of man must mean the development of that kind of society which serves man, which enhances his wellbeing and preserves his dignity.

Thus the development of peoples involves economic development, social development and political development. And at this time in man's history it must imply a divine discontent and a determination for change. For the present condition of men must be unacceptable to all who think of an individual person as a unique creation of a living God. We say man is created in the image of God. I refuse to imagine a God who is poor, ignorant, superstitious, fearful, oppressed, wretched . . . which is the lot of the majority of those He created in His own image. Men are creators of themselves and their conditions, but under present conditions we are creatures not of God but our fellowmen.[23]

Nyerere sees socialism as the necessary expression of development in Middle Africa, not because it delivers an economic utopia but because it proclaims interdependence between people as the means and goal of development. God acts not in overthrowing oppressor classes but in building a new partnership of strong and weak, between nations and within a nation where no group holds power over any other group. We locate Nyerere's position close to humanization on the spectrum but nearer liberation.

The second theology of development in Africa is also a form of humanization and liberation. In Southern Africa the context of poverty is closely linked with race. South African theologians of liberation identify racist policies as the means which prevent black people from realizing their God-given potential and from exercizing control over their destiny. This racism is theologically defended and justified but distorts humanity. Manas Butheleze writes: "Colonized humanity (is) a state of existence in which the self-hood becomes alienated from its 'human house' — the self-hood is placed under house-arrest."[24] New images of God are needed to counteract the image of authoritarian dominance purveyed by white man's religion. Ananias Mpynize writes: "People (are) made in the image of the Trinity, among whose three persons there is no superiority, and are not meant to set some up in authority over others to rule their lives. This theology says that man, with his longing for fellowship, will tear down every structure that sets about trying to rule over others."[25]

These theologians do not however discuss the methods by which God or the church will bring this liberation into practice.

The late Byang Kato was executive secretary of the Association of Evangelicals of Africa and Madagascar (AEAM) and Chairman of the Theological Commission of the World Evangelical Fellowship. He endorses the Black Theologians' perspective of the situation in Africa.

Enslavement of Africans by the whites is probably the worst evil done by one class of people to another. It may be surpassed only by Hitler's massacre of six million Jews. Until about 20 years ago, American blacks experienced many kinds of humiliation on account of the pigmentation of their skin. Today (Jan. 1976) 250,000 whites are lording it over the 5 million African Rhodesians on the false pretext that they are preserving Christian civilization. In apartheid South Africa today, the Soweto black town dweller works to provide comfort for the white suburban inhabitants of ultra-modern Johannesburg, but is denied the fruit of his labour. To keep the black man in perpetual bondage, the racist regime is reported to spend about 5,000 shillings a year for the education of an average white child and about 300 shillings for a black child . . . Injustice of this type is one of the evils that have given rise to Black Theology.[26]

Kato identifies the analysis of the late Steve Biko as Hegelian. He quotes him: "The thesis is in fact a strong white racism, and therefore the antithesis to this must, ipso facto, be a strong solidarity among the blacks, on whom this white racism seeks to prey. Out of these two situations we can therefore hope to reach some kind of balance — a true humanity where power politics will have no place."[27] Kato prefers the prescription of an African theologian of the past, Tertullian.

Tertullian declared: "Christians are members of the third race." Just as it is wrong for any Christian to support racial prejudice and oppression, so it is wrong for the black Christian to lump all whites into one category and condemn them all. Rather than pitting thesis against antithesis on the basis of race, Christians from belligerent camps should stand as the synthesis, with Jesus Christ as the head of the newly-created body (Ephesians 4:15).[28]

Kato rejects the concepts of Black Theology, but reckons that its questions set the agenda for biblical study. "I appeal to my Christian brothers, Africans and non-Africans, to search the Scriptures, and stand by Scriptural principles. According to the Scriptures believers, under any human condition, are already liberated. 'For freedom Christ has set us free' (Galatians 5:1). But our freedom in Christ should challenge us to seek for justice through peaceful means."[29]

A third approach to development identifies the key issue as human dignity. Africans must be allowed to express their Christian faith within the framework of their African culture. Tite Tienou, the secretary of the Theological Commission of the AEAM, writes: "The necessity to integrate Christianity with African culture runs like an Ariadne thread in Mbiti and other African writers: it has been felt as far back as the second half of the nineteenth century by people like Mojola Agbebi. One would have thought that we were beyond stressing the need and into specifics."[30] He regards Mbiti as the spokesman for African theology. Mbiti writes:

Culture is the human pattern of life in response to man's environment; . . . the only lasting form of Christianity in this continent is that which results from a serious encounter of the Gospel with the indigenous African culture when the people voluntarily accept by faith the Gospel of Jesus Christ. A Christianity which is heavily intertwined with an imported culture may indeed be very impressive, but it cannot be a substitute for this kind of Christianity, that should grow out of the spontaneous free impregnation of the Gospel in the fertile womb of African culture . . . What is the message of the Gospel to our culture in the areas of human problems and needs, such as oppression, exploitation, poverty, starvation, injustice, destruction of human life, extravagant spoliation of nature, pollution and dangers to human survival (such as armaments, wars, domination, even science and technology)? How can the Gospel raise an alarm through our culture in these areas of urgent concern?[31]

Tienou grasps the hub of Mbiti's concern when he writes in review of one of his articles, "Is there only one cultural mode of doing theology? Or are we from the so-called Third World the only ones to make the jump from one cultural heritage to another which is thought (consciously or unconsciously) to be universal?"[32] Mbiti voices the frustration of encountering one dominant cultural method of doing theology which claims universal validity when he writes that Christian scholars in Europe and North America "have more academic fellowship with heretics long dead than with living brethren of the Church today in the so-called Third World."[33] Tienou and Mbiti here echo a concern that now arises from all round the world: western theology does not have the universal validity that it has claimed. Using biblical criteria, it must examine the cultural presuppositions that underlie it. It will often have its eyes opened to these criteria as it listens to the theologizing of those in other cultures. Choan-Seng Song expresses this in these words:

Black Theology in the United States and Africa, Latin American theology of liberation and feminist theology have made at least two things become crystal clear. First: each theological formulation, be it that of the venerable church father or that of impressive German theology, is historically and culturally conditioned and this must be appreciated and critiqued as such. It has no automatic claim to universal authority. Transplanted into other historical and cultural contexts, it must be tested. Untested credal or theological formulation is no better than rote-learning. It will not take root in the soil in which faith must struggle to grow. And, second, each theology must be judged primarily on its own merits and not in competition with other systems of theology. The decisiveness of the Christian gospel consists partly in the fact that it has a particular message in a particular situation. Once this particularity is set aside, the cutting edge of the Gospel becomes blunt and harmless.[34]

The implications of this for theology of development is that we must recognize that God acts through his people in different cultures to raise serious questions on the practice of his people in other cultures; and this traffic of questioning is not one-way. No one culture can offer a theology of development to another culture, not only because human dignity requires that the people of the culture work out their own understanding of Christian development in dialogue with the Scriptures, but because the theological expression of the dominant culture may be itself dominated by non-biblical motifs.

Such questioning is taking place in the theologizing of the

Lutheran church in South Africa and may be described as the fourth theology of development in Africa.

Klaus Nurnberger edits an impressive collection of statistical analysis and biblical exegesis entitled *Affluence, Poverty and the Word of God.*[35] Using the Lutheran division of Law and Gospel he identifies as Law all self-justification in development. The liberation model identifies the rich as culprits, the poor as victims; the poor will one day take what is theirs. On the other hand the modernization model blames the poor as lazy, assures the rich they have only what they deserve and that the poor can have some of it if they work hard enough. God essentially acts through the church to expose *both* self-justifications and proclaim a via media where the rich begin to share and the poor to achieve. Nurnberger describes the two models in these terms:

The modernization model says: "The poor have been left behind on the road of progress":

Followers of the modernization model have more or less the following picture of the development problem. Their basic assumption is that history moves in one direction towards ever greater achievements and fulfilment. Some societies and especially some groups of people within societies are far advanced on this common road: others have been left behind. The advanced are so far ahead because they have developed a rational outlook on life, a scientific and technical mentality, new ways for the utilization of available resources, sophisticated and powerful means of production, smooth and fast channels of trade and communication, efficient administrative and financial institutions and the like. Their planned utilization of scientific research and technological innovation and their successful investment of the accumulating capital for productive ends has led to a rapid growth of their economic capacity, standard of living, power and influence. The others have been left behind on this road to success. Some have not even made up their mind to start walking yet. They have a mentality or culture which is directed towards communal sharing and the enjoyment of fellowship rather than to individual achievement; towards supernatural powers rather than to an empirical and utilitarian view of nature; towards an ever valid past rather than towards a future which needs to be conquered. Their techniques are simple, their distribution practices irrational, their institutions archaic and untrustworthy, their administration according to corrupt patterns. There is no accumulation and utilization of productive capital. The result is, inevitably, a poor economic performance. If you add a rapid growth of the population which cancels out any progress immediately, you have all the ingredients for the spread of stagnation and misery. To remedy this situation, this model suggests that our main task is to make the economy of the backward societies grow fast by offering strong material incentives for achievement, by applying science and technology, by generating productive capital, by developing efficient administrative and financial institutions and means of communication, by creating a rational mentality, by arresting population growth — in short by "modernizing" the whole set-up from top to toe. Because of their superior knowledge and experience, the advanced should help the backward on this ladder of progress through educational, technological and scientific aid, and through the investment of some of their spare capital in the backward economy so that it gets going in the direction of growth. It is believed in these circles that this process has forcefully been initiated during the colonial era but that it needs to be accelerated by the new leadership of the former colonies which owes its existence, sophistication and drive to the impact of western civilization.[36]

The rich favour the modernization model: the poor are bound to resent it:
The modernization model is very flattering for the rich. On top of all their economic privileges, social prestige and political power, the model endows them with moral status as well. It gives them the assurance that they only have what they deserve. The ingenuity and diligence of their fathers have achieved something which previous generations and their own contemporaries were unable to attain. They themselves are able to preserve and forcefully enhance this heritage through professional expertize, hard work and goal-directed thinking. Having advanced far ahead of others on the common road, they find themselves in the status of fatherly advisers and helpers, if not in the position of natural leaders. The model enhances their self-image all round and nowhere questions their identity or integrity. It would be a miracle if they did not readily embrace the explanations which this model offers.

With the poor the situation is completely different. On top of all their misery the model makes them bear all the blame for their inferior position. Modern western society is built on the achievement norm which they are unable to satisfy. Which means that their moral integrity is questioned. They are considered to be dull, lazy, incompetent, disorganized, inefficient and the like. At best they are the objects of pity to whom alms have to be given, or they are considered to be immature and need to be led by others. At worst they are left in their deserved misery, so that they may come to their senses and start to do something about it. It is a thoroughly humiliating picture. There are many poor people who have adopted this explanation and accepted the implied judgment. This in turn frequently means that they lose all self-respect and self-confidence. They become despondent and fatalistic. Those who are 'conscientized', on the other hand, cannot help but hate, reject and fight this model.[37]

The role of the church is to analyze critically the presence of such self-justification in attempts at development. God acts as judge of all humanisms. The church has the prophetic role of exposing these 'isms' because it is liberated from false self-justification. Its role is also to seek "a model or interpretation which enables us to see all the relevant aspects of the problem in their proper perspective, directs each and every person to the tasks which fall within his own sphere of responsibility and competence, and formulates concrete goals which can realistically be taken as guide-lines for action in the right direction."[38] Such a model should aim at a proper balance between natural resources, economic activity and population numbers. This theology has affinities with liberation and humanization but we locate it nearer modernization.

Western Europe and North America

As we surveyed the history of Christian reflection in our historical survey, we noted the beginning of the Protestant missionary movement from the western church at the end of the eighteenth century. This movement gave birth to churches in Asia and Africa, and started Protestant churches in Latin America. It is in these churches, started through a movement from the western church, that the present issues of the debate about where God is at work in the world have been sharply raised.

During the colonial and missionary era of the nineteenth and early twentieth century there was little uncertainty in any of the western or missionary churches about where God was at work. He was at work in the expansion of the church in the world. The church educated good citizens who lived as salt in society. Theological reflection by churches in the missionary lands was by and large limited to understanding and consuming the theological reflection of the sending churches which was presumed to be universally valid.

The age of colonialism passed and the new situations in independent countries led the churches there to ask questions of the Christian traditions they had received. As the newly independent nations assumed responsibility for their own social, political and economic problems, those who had attained political power by leading the struggle against foreign rulers, now had to maintain power by winning the fight against what was perceived as the misfortune of poverty. The churches also had to establish their credibility in this situation. They had a legacy of being closely identified with the foreign rulers. Now they had to establish their loyalty to the aspirations of the new nation. So the churches joined in the task of nation-building through the traditional means of building schools and hospitals.

But poverty did not go away. As we have seen, some Christian theologians, in what was now termed the Third World, began to reflect on the causes for this. They reflected on the structural links that their nations continued to have with the west, which were partly a legacy of their colonial past. They concluded that these structures needed changing and sought for a theology of structural social change. And so liberation theology came to birth in the churches founded by the missionary movement. The major focus of the church's reflection has been to define the activity of God in relation to efforts to change the social realities which lie beneath the poverty and injustice which permeate their societies.

It is among the offspring of the western sending churches that this theological concern for structural social change has arisen as a major issue. As we trace the experience of the sending churches themselves in their own cultures, we perceive an interaction with the socio-economic realities of the day, but no such radical criticism or concern for structural change.

The age of colonialism and missionary expansion in the west grew alongside the tremendous expansion brought about by the industrial revolution in the eighteenth and nineteenth centuries. The social philosophy underlying this revolution was the enlightened self-interest of rationalism, whose economic expression was capitalism. Its progenitor was Adam Smith, who thought he could identify self-interest as the motor for social development.

Every individual is continually exerting himself to find the most advantageous employment for whatever capital he can command. It is his own advantage, indeed, and not that of society, which he has in view. But the study of his own advantage naturally, or rather necessarily, leads him to prefer that employment which is most advantageous to the society.[39]

"Serve yourself and the community will benefit" was the moral alchemy which would turn the grossest self-interest into the pure gold of social progress. All moral questions of justice were dissolved into the solvent of enlightened self-interest.

Christian faith interacted with this in many ways. Some saw capitalism as the natural expression of the Protestant work ethic; others saw it as the work of an immanental evolutionary God of social progress. God was at work building up creation. Essentially this school saw the roots of capitalism in the Christian faith.

However, since the nineteenth century a section of Christian opinion in the church has identified the roots of capitalism in

non-Christian views of man and economic life (e.g. unbridled
self-interest and utilitarianism measured in terms of individual
preferences).[40] They saw God at work in the church mitigating
the effects of capitalism. Many Christian social work groups
provided housing, clothes and education for poor people. One
group of Christians began to criticize the operation of capitalism itself by the ethics of Jesus. These Christians have been
misnamed as supporters of a Social Gospel. But John Bennett
writes that the advocates of the Social Gospel were "in no sense
abandoning the individual Gospel but were insisting that a partial Gospel should become a whole Gospel and that the religion
of Jesus should become regnant in all the activities of men."[41]

A representative of this school shows that they were not
utopian idealists. F. Ernest Johnson wrote in 1935,

At every point the church is confronted by the issue of method in
promoting social change . . . Devotion to 'principles' without regard
to specific situations and predictable results is not rugged morality but
obscurantism. In the existing economic situation a struggle is always
going on between privilege and need, and violence is deeply embedded
in the economic structure. There is a pitiable unreality in the average
person's attitude toward conflict between social groups. He habitually
begins his scrutiny at the point where the outbreak occurs. The deep
and silent causes of conflict which lie in unjust social arrangements
that make the mass of men dependent upon a few, to their own
material and cultural disadvantage — these causes commonly go un-
recognized. We have heard much of non-violent resistance as an
ethical method, but there is an evil form of overtly non-violent resistance by entrenched privilege which can afford to forgo aggression.[42]

The Social Gospel writers discerned that the genius of American business concentrated too exclusively on the problems of
production and not enough on solving social problems. In 1908
the Federal Council of the Churches of Christ adopted the
Social Creed of the Churches. This proclaimed that the
churches must stand "for equal right and complete justice for
all men in all stations of life", "for the most equitable division
of the product of industry that can ultimately be devised"; in
1912 the creed was amended to include the "right of employees
and employers alike to organize".[43]

In Britain the Nonconformist movement had given birth to
labour unions to achieve countervailing power in negotiations
with employers. Keir Hardie, the founder of the Labour Party,
the unions' political wing, was a devout Christian, and a Bishop
of Durham supported the Durham Miners' Strike.

So some western Christians discerned God's activity in the

church in judging and mitigating the worst effects of capitalism. The church's prophetic ministry at the turn of the century proved effective. Enlightened capitalists such as Lord Rank, Lord Nuffield, Henry Ford and Lord Thompson combined business brilliance with social concern.[44] The welfare state developed with capitalist society. So the capitalist picture changed completely from the days of the industrial revolution. The contemporary model of capitalism now combines social care with opportunities for freedom and growth.

But the theological basis for this prophetic criticism was progressively undermined. The criticism of capitalism was based initially on the ethics of Jesus. However rationalistic and humanistic understandings of Scripture undermined the claim of this approach to objective authority. Rationalistic understandings of religion as subjective feeling (Schleiermacher) also undermined authority for valid criticism of society. Niebuhr further undermined the theological basis of the social gospel. He suspected it of utopian idealism and emphasized the Christian doctrine of sin in place of the Christian doctrine of hope.

So a number of factors lead the majority of western Christians today to take the contemporary capitalist model as the only Christian alternative for development. First, capitalism has succeeded in combining economic growth, personal freedom and social concern in the western world. Secondly, the questions about capitalism raised by the church at the turn of the century seemed theologically suspect because of the attacks of people like Niebuhr. Therefore the church seems to accept increasingly the Weber-Tawney thesis that the ethical roots of capitalism lie in the Christian doctrines of man and work.[45]

As a result, the west in general and western churches in particular see capitalism as the model for development in the Third World. The questions of the prophetic movement at the turn of the century, however, are now being asked in a more fundamental form by Christians in the Third World, and a few radical groups in the west. They see capitalism in the legacy of the western world in their own countries, in industries and in multinational corporations. They see firms employing people under exploitative conditions, producing goods for a small minority in their own country and for export, in order to gain foreign exchange to purchase luxury goods for the same small minority, or at best to purchase food for survival from the western food mountains. They see the dichotomy of the labour practices of the multinationals between their factories in the west and their factories in the Third World. They begin to wonder whether the success of capitalism in the west in combining welfare with self-interest has not been bought at the price of poverty in the Third World. They think that Gunder Frank has a prima facie case when he states that capitalism has not abolished poverty from the west, but exported it.[46]

Within the west itself a small group of Christian economists, prompted by the questions of the Third World, are re-examining the ethical basis of capitalism by Christian principles.[47] For example, Stephen Mott writes:

Capitalism's proposal to take account of human sin by counter-balancing the self-interest of the individual with the self-interests of others is wholly inadequate, when judged by biblical principles . . . Sin does not take care of itself; it produces no social harmonies. It seeks advantage in the least advantage of power and the least crack of weakness, and there grows and destroys. The Social Darwinism behind capitalism is responsible for the idea that in the social struggle the rich are the more competent and more virtuous and the poor are the losers by reason of their lack of ambition and ability . . . Equality of opportunity thus means only that the same procedures should be applied to the poor and the rich. Capitalist theory assumes that society improves by the process in which the strong gain power and the weak go to the bottom . . . (Therefore) even well meaning governmental interference with natural selection will produce a sick and weakened society. Welfare and other social programmes bring people to a level higher than they can maintain, weakening the whole for only a temporary benefit to the naturally weak. Such a view of government is far from the biblical view of justice as taking up the cause of the weak, rather than ensuring the superiority of the powerful. The biblical ideal of the ruler is not a kind uncle smiling his approval on his battling nieces and nephews as long as they do not break any rules. Rather the ideal is the ruler who "crushes the oppressor and gives deliverance to the needy" (Ps. 72:4).[48]

Mott closes with a line from Charles Dickens: "Every man for himself and God for all, shouted the elephant as he danced among the chickens." Such judgments are also to be found in the work of Alan Storkey, Donald Hay, E. F. Schumacher and Tony Cramp who are Christians and economists of standing.

Amidst this questioning, third world Christians are asking the west to understand their cries. They are asking whether western theology preserves the status quo and whether it is adequate or biblical. They are searching for a theology of social change which will not only relieve the symptoms of their poverty but tackle its causes in social structures.

CHAPTER THREE
Toward a Theology of Social Change

3

Toward a Theology of Social Change

VINAY SAMUEL and CHRIS SUGDEN

Theologies and Strategies for Development

Christian commitment to action in the world involves struggle in society. Struggle arises out of Christian understanding of the world, which is in rebellion against God and is the arena of his activity, loved by him. In each situation struggle is involved in moving society from what it is to what it ought to be. The Third World identifies that struggle as one between the strong and weak in society; the First World sees the struggle as a struggle to master God-given resources in nature. The First World tends to downplay the struggle between the strong and the weak in Third World societies because the First World has gradually developed checks and balances to produce countervailing power to limit the strong in their own societies.

In the three continents of the Third World, Christians are developing theologies and programmes for struggle against oppressive political and/or oppressive economic systems. In Latin America the context is struggle against oppressive governments and economic systems. They advocate a programme for the church to become educated about the rights of the poor, side with the poor, awake them to their rights and organize them to exercize countervailing power to achieve those rights. There is no disagreement over the central role of the church in the struggle. There is considerable debate about whether Christians can use violence. Everyone agrees that there is covert violence of the strong against the weak. Some from a Thomistic tradition regard that as grounds for legitimate self-defence by the weak in a just revolution; others stress that Jesus taught non-violence in resisting enemies and overcoming evil in society.

In Asia the struggle is also against oppressive political and economic systems, often reinforced by religion. In many parts of Asia, violence is not an option for Christian obedience, because of the teaching of the gospel, the minority status of the church, and the religious and social traditions of non-violence in the cultures. But the place of the church in social change is under sharp debate. For thinkers like M. M. Thomas the church is less relevant. God's action is taking place in society and the church is being formed wherever humanization occurs. Those loyal to Jesus Christ should find him in these 'open Churches'. For evangelicals like Vinay Samuel and Chris Sugden, the church is central in any Christian social programme, as a model of what society ought to be like, a catalyst for achieving that goal, and the goal of God's redemptive work in society in Christ. To achieve this end the church should engage in educating its members in issues of justice, making the poor aware of their rights, working with the poor in projects where the poor have maximum participation, and sharing in partnership with the world-wide church to achieve these ends.

In Africa the struggle is mainly against oppressive economic systems. In states such as Tanzania the government is itself committed to changing economic structures for the benefit of the poorest. So struggle is more formalized in political and educational institutions. People are encouraged in participation, self-reliance and community organization by the government itself. In South Africa the picture is different. The struggle is against an oppressive government which is seen as the source of racist and oppressive economic policies. South African theologians of liberation have not yet spelt out their programme, but their theology implies the struggle of the weak to attain the rights of human beings.

What methods should Christians use in the struggle between the poor and weak to move society to where it ought to be? There are a number of ethical options on which Christians in the Third World share common ground. They agree that the church should follow her master in identifying her concerns, her interests and her lifestyle with the poor, weak and oppressed in society over against the rich and the strong. The church should clearly take the side of the poor in society, not because the poor will always be right but because they are most likely to be taken advantage of and be unprotected against those who would exploit them. The church should make the poor aware of their rights and dignity as human beings, informed both by her own understanding of the dignity of man, and by the rights enshrined in national and international declarations, which spell out justice in society. The church should work for change in the political and economic systems, so that there is room for the poor both to attain and to exercize their legitimate rights.

How should the church work for change in the political and economic systems? Here there is a clear difference of opinion. One school of thought identifies the problem as the exercize of power in society. Society is controlled by those who are enabled by their wealth, status, and followings to hold the levers of power. Christians should work with all groups who are seeking to gain those levers of power and try to operate them for the benefit of the poorest. If only a violent contest will remove the current holders of the levers of power from their positions, then Christians must not shrink from that necessity. They will be theologically fortified by a long tradition in western theology of legitimate Christian participation in just war and tyrannicide.

A second school of thought begins with the demonstration of God's power in the New Testament through the powerlessness of Christ in his ministry and finally on the cross. During his ministry he renounced worldly power and spectacular displays of supernatural power. He moved among the powerless and exploited people of society and associated with those of low social status. He made himself vulnerable to jibes of illegitimacy and drunkenness, and had nowhere to lay his head. This display of the nature of God's power in servanthood provoked the vested interests of Jewish society to have him crucified. The crucifixion saw Jesus at his most powerless in the world's terms. But as the suffering servant he opened the way for the unstoppable resurrection power of God to burst in on human history through his resurrection from the dead thus confirming his Lordship over history. While the natural working of human power in the world produces distortions in society which bring injustice and suffering, God shows his power to correct and redeem these in the cross where Jesus took the consequences of men's distorted use of power. The New Testament affirms not that Jesus had no power whatsoever, but that Jesus displayed the true power of God as he renounced worldly forms of power and lived, died and rose as the suffering servant.[1]

The church is to be the community where this same power of God is demonstrated as she takes the same role as her master. The Acts and Epistles show that God's power is active as barriers are broken down in human relationships and new relationships of justice and peace are built. Gentiles enter the infant Christian communities on the same footing as Jews. Masters and slaves, husbands and wives are mutually subordinate to

each other. These barriers are broken and these new relationships are built through repentance and forgiveness, through
reconciliation in place of retaliation.

The church today is called to demonstrate this true power of
God by learning the powerlessness and servanthood of Jesus.
She should renounce worldly models of growth and success, and
take the side of the socially oppressed, the poor and those who
have no place in their own society. She should build relationships and structures in her own life and practice which challenge
the prevailing injustices in the society around her. The church
should also be engaged in promoting those structures in society
which attempt to bring just relationships, and should be engaged in evangelism to share Jesus Christ as the one who makes
them possible. In a recent meeting of Christians with Hindu
businessmen discussion centred on whether it was possible to be
humane and just in employment practices and at the same time
make a profit. The concluding question was "How is it possible
for self-centred men to become humane and just?"

The church will also seek to demonstrate ways in which the
weak and the strong can be related in ways which neither continue the weak in false dependence on the paternalism of the
strong, nor recruit a few members for the strong from among
the weak, but achieve the goal of equality. This model must
develop both within society, within national churches and
between churches in the third and first worlds.

In the western world we discern three strategies for Christian
action. The first strategy is of those western theologians who
identify themselves closely with liberation theology.[2] They call
for a new international order and for radical changes within the
western nations, not only to change the consumer patterns
which determine international economics, but also to give justice to those groups whom they perceive as oppressed within the
west: blacks, women, immigrants, and those in declining industries and neighbourhoods. This group of theologians would
especially include Martin Luther King and James Cone. Martin
Luther King's actions and writings eloquently demonstrated the
potential of a non-violent Christian critique of and resistance to
endemic structural injustice, in the form of racism. His life and
writings have long been an inspiration to both authors of this
paper. James Cone has contributed a forceful critique of American society and of American theology, and done important
work on how culture conditions biblical interpretation. Both
these contributors must be taken especial notice of because they
offer their critique from a non-Marxist stance, though of course

many of their detractors would disagree with that.[3]

Western theologians of similar sympathies now call on the Western churches to support liberation groups in Third World churches. This strategy clearly surfaced at the Uppsala assembly of the W.C.C. in 1968. The Programme to Combat Racism was formed as a mode of Christian obedience to alter the structures of racist Christian societies.

The second strategy is of those who identify the struggle in the Third World as a struggle to master God-given resources in nature. They advocate an enlightened capitalism as the way to win in this struggle, developing individual initiative and providing those resources that are lacking. They choose this path for a number of reasons. First, they see the success of enlightened capitalism in the west. Secondly, social struggle within the the west between the strong and the weak was carried on by and large within democratic frameworks and within the spirit of the Christian tradition where an appeal was always possible to the conscience of the strong. They do not see the priority of social struggle in the Third World. Thirdly, they suspect that issues of a struggle would involve the church in an improper and unchristian commitment to certain political stances.

We also discern a third group in the west who are distinct from the first two groups, and are gradually formulating a distinct theology and strategy. Those in this group are all evangelical, but have different roots.

In America Anabaptist Christians felt that the Anabaptist heritage had an important witness to the wider church which seemed to be flirting with violence to produce social change in response to the problems posed by liberation theologians. The Anabaptist tradition combined concern for structural change in society through new structures in the church with a commitment to non-violence. John Yoder's *Politics of Jesus* comes from this tradition and became a seminal book for many who were asking for biblical guidelines for structural change when it appeared in 1972.[4]

The Vietnam experience prompted Jim Wallis and others in what is now the Sojourners' Community to question the marriage between Christianity and the American dream which had appeared to sanction the Vietnamese war as a defence of Christian faith and values.[5]

These groups joined with those from more traditional reformed backgrounds such as Carl Henry to produce the Chicago Declaration in 1973.

In Britain in the late sixties the Shaftesbury Project of the

Inter-Varsity Fellowship, and The Evangelical Alliance Relief
Fund of the Evangelical Alliance (TEAR Fund) began to
develop practical projects for harnessing increasing evangelical
discussion on social issues into concrete action. Many other
small groups had been pursuing evangelical social concern,[6] but
these national movements put the social question firmly on the
evangelical agenda.

At Lausanne in 1974, Rene Padilla and Samuel Escobar
brought the question of social justice into the centre of evangelical debate. Concern for social justice was expressed in the formal
Covenant, but a large number of conference members produced
a further statement strengthening the commitment to social
justice in the mission of the church. Since then a major debate
has begun in evangelical circles on the place of social justice in
the mission of the church. *Christian Mission in the Modern
World* by John Stott,[7] and *Rich Christians in an Age of Hunger*
by Ron Sider[8] have been important trend-setting books in the
evangelical community in the last few years.

This response by evangelicals has produced a lot of social
concern, involvement, sacrificial giving, development projects
and attempts at simpler lifestyle. But it has not produced a
coherent theology of social change adequate to deal with the
questions of structural change raised by theologians of liberation. So most evangelicals in the First World and their partners
in Third World churches are largely found in category two of
the strategies we discern. They also follow theology number 2 of
the three theologies of social change that we outline.

Towards a Theology of Social Change

What development strategies arise out of the two understandings of Christian involvement in development that we examined?

Understanding one, that development activity expresses
God's work in providence, issues in a strategy of disinterested
concern in the welfare of society as a whole. The Lausanne
Covenant gives succinct expression to this theology.

We affirm that God is both the Creator and the Judge of all men. We
therefore should share his concern for justice and reconciliation
throughout human society, and for liberation of men from all kinds of
oppression. Because man is made in the image of God, every person...
has an intrinsic dignity, because of which he should be respected and
served, not exploited.[9]

Christian involvement in development comes under the man-
date of creation. It is the activity of the kingdom of God's left

hand. Christians act as salt and light in the world in their call-
ings in secular society, to preserve a just human and social
order. This theology of development extends Christian strategy
to education, health, agriculture and other projects which
enhance the dignity of man.

A leading advocate of this theology is John R. W. Stott. He
writes: "God the creator is constantly active in his world in providence, in common grace and in judgment, quite apart from
the purposes for which he has sent his Son, his Spirit and his
church into the world."[10] In other words God sustains and
judges in the world, quite separately from his redemptive work
in Christ. The redemptive work of Christ is limited to where
Christ is consciously acknowledged and that can be only in the
church, not even in a 'Christian' nation. This means that any
true change towards God's purpose for man in society, arising
out of the death and resurrection of Christ, can take place only
within the confines of the church.[11] This is the root of the tension in evangelical discussion between evangelism and social
action; since the acknowledgement of Christ is always required
for any true social change, evangelism always has a priority.

Third World Christians, including many evangelicals, are
asking that the church around the world address itself to the
problems of social change and the issues of struggle between the
strong and the weak to achieve a just society. Those in the First
World who have partner churches in the Third World favour a
strategy of struggle to master natural resources, based on a theology where God is seen as the creator, preserver and judge of
the natural order. Such a theology is in the eyes of some inadequate for grappling with the burning issues of social change and
struggle between the weak and the strong.

Our fundamental criticism of this 'creation-based theology' is
that it is divorced from redemption, from the eschatological re-
capitulation of all things in Christ which has been inaugurated
with his coming. Our criticisms of the effects of this theology
are therefore not to be taken as criticisms of the place of
creation in Christian theologizing, but of a defective theology of
creation divorced from eschatological salvation which is present
now.

First, such a defective theology of creation gives no basis for
identifying, entering or directing struggle between weak and
strong. It sees the church only as a sign-post and conscience for
society, speaking out prophetically against injustice and bad
stewardship, setting a standard for society, and modelling what
the church ought to be like. Secondly, without the eschatologi-

cal dimension, the bias of the theology is for preserving the created order while the real task of redemption takes place on the 'spiritual' level. This gives little encouragement for social change and tends to help the status quo. God is identified as the author and preserver of the status quo, he preserves it, he will at the end of history judge it, but he does not change it now. This theological position becomes an unwitting ally of the status quo. Thirdly, such a defective creation theology can easily slip into a dualism: since the real sphere of God's activity is the spiritual sphere, creation and the created can be lower on the Christian agenda than it should be. Christian activity and action are directed more towards the expansion of the church. Costly involvement in issues of struggle which might hamper numerical growth is often missing from the church's witness.

Happily many people are better than their theologies and do not act consistently with their theologies. This makes it all the more imperative to develop a sound theological base for activity for social change, which Christian churches and agencies in the Third World are discerning as increasingly imperative if biblical justice is to be achieved. We wish to suggest that the Bible does not in fact stop at theology number 1, the theology which separates God's role in the world as creator, preserver and judge from his role in the church as redeemer. We suggest that biblical teaching supports the view that the struggle to achieve just relationships between the weak and the strong in society is not a secondary activity of the church. It is an application of the redemptive work of God in Christ to the world outside the church. In support of this view we cite a number of key biblical themes.

The kingdom of God

God is at work in the world in establishing his kingdom through Jesus Christ. An increasing body of literature is exploring and developing the theme of the kingdom of God in the gospels and its central place in the mission of Jesus and in the mission of the church.[12] We are beginning to see that the scope of the kingdom of God extends not just to the community of the King that consciously acknowledges Jesus as Lord, but is also seen in God's kingdom activity in the world beyond the church. The kingdom of God is seen not only as God calls men in repentance and faith to join the church, but also as the just relationships that belong to the kingdom are established in society. These just relationships are seen clearly in Jesus' own ministry, as he announces the kingdom as good news to the poor, as he declares that the bias of the kingdom is to invite the outcast and the oppressed to the king's feast, as he castigates the religious leaders for ignoring justice, as he gives a priority to the poor, sick and oppressed in his ministry.

There is a broad sense of agreement about the nature of God's kingdom activity. But other biblical themes need further exploration in order to provide clarity in understanding the scope of God's kingdom activity. We would like to dwell on these other themes.

The world

God's kingdom activity has to do with the world God made. What is the world that God is at work in? The Bible has a double focus in discussing the world. The world is man-in-society in rebellion against God, the usage reflected in the term 'worldly'. Paul advises that we should not be conformed to this world. The rebellion of the world finds its climax, reveals its nature and experiences complete defeat in the cross of Jesus. Paul writes in Galatians 6:14 "By means of his cross, the world is dead to me, and I am dead to the world."

Secondly, the world is the arena of God's activity. It is loved by him and destined not for final abandonment but to be transformed into God's kingdom at the return of Christ in a new heaven and new earth.[13]

From this theme we discern that God has a purpose for the world outside the church in his plan of redemption. If his plan of redemption is being put into partial effect now, that redemption could be at work in the world beyond the church.

God at work in Christ

God's kingdom activity is focussed in, and inaugurated by Jesus Christ. The New Testament witness is that the God of the Jews is to be understood as the God and Father of our Lord Jesus Christ; that the work of God in creation and redemption is focussed, defined and executed in Christ.[14] The theological question that this raises is whether God works in the world at present apart from what he has shown of himself in Christ. Does God work on the basis of Christ's death and resurrection only in the church? Has the victory of Christ over sin, evil and death in his cross and resurrection no implications for the way God works in the world as a whole outside the church? Of course, conscious acknowledgement of that victory takes place

in the church, and salvation in its full sense is linked with that
conscious acknowledgement. But are the effects of Christ's victory limited only to where it is consciously acknowledged in the
world? Does his victory not have any implications for the work
of God in the world beyond the church? If we say that it has no
implications or effects, then we are saying that God works in the
world outside the church, without relationship to the victory of
Christ on the cross. If, however, God's whole work in the world
is related to the death and resurrection of Christ, we may look
for the pattern of redemption at work where God is at work in
the world beyond the church. We can say that God does more
than preserve and judge the world outside the church; he works
to change it into conformity with his redemption plan. This
theme is a Christological theme.

God at work in law and promise

If God works in the world beyond the church to apply the
results of the victory of the cross, how does he do so? The
answer we suggest lies in his Law and his promise.[15] God's kingdom activity is in fulfilment of his promise and to establish his
Law. In the Old Testament God worked among his people and
the nations through two agents — the Law and the promise. The
Law was given to the people who inherited God's promise to
Abraham; it was part of the promise. The Law defined God's
expectations of his people in establishing just and human relationships in society. The Law was meant to prevent structures
from exploiting and oppressing the poor, to provide protection
and relief for the poor and vulnerable. The Law was God's instrument of judgment for Israel. It was also his instrument of
judgment for the nations. The Old Testament prophets held the
surrounding nations guilty by the standards of God's Law.[16]

God's work through promise was his intervention in grace to
bring renewal. His action in promise delivered Israel from Egypt
and made possible a new beginning in the promised land. His
promise prevented Israel's complete destruction and in spite of
her constant apostasy God used his people to manifest his Son.

Law was not separate from promise. Both worked together.
Law did not block the way for people realizing the need for the
promise. Both Law and promise, judgment and grace, went together. The gift of the Law was part of the fulfilment of God's
promise to deliver his people and give them a land where they
could worship and serve him. Jonah's announcement of God's
Law and judgment to Nineveh contained the possibility of pro-

mise and grace, much to Jonah's surprise and annoyance. Amos insisted that the Israelites were not the only ones who had experienced God's hand in a national exodus: "Did I not bring up the Philistines from Caphtor and the Syrians from Kir?"[17] God's work of Law and promise, judgment and grace, is neither indiscriminately universal, nor yet confined to Israel.

The Law and the promise are fulfilled in Christ — supremely in his atoning death. He fulfils the demands of the Law, for disobedient humanity and gives the decisive interpretation of the Law. In his death he took the full penalty of the Law on himself, in accepting God's judgment on sin; yet this was at the same time the fulfilment of God's promise of a new covenant. Jesus fulfilled the promise of Isaiah 61:1-4. Law and promise, judgment and grace are united in the invasion of God's kingdom into history. Jesus exercized a ministry of judgment on Israel in his prophetic denunciation of the Jewish leaders, and offered grace and shalom to God's covenant people: "Would that even today you knew the things that make for peace."[18] He called a community to be the sign of the kingdom by demonstrating God's action of Law and promise in their life. The community was to exhibit in her economic, social and political life the operation of God's Law and promise, breaking down and building up, putting to death and renewing.

If God's Law is so closely linked with his promise, can we describe God as at work outside the church in the world as judge without bringing some aspect of promise? The purpose of his Law in the Old Testament was to prevent structures from exploiting the poor and to provide protection and relief for the poor and vulnerable. The Law was not an instrument of condemnation without hope. It did not preserve the status quo, but sought to change it and open it up for the ultimate acceptance of God's promise.

God at work in judgment and grace

God's kingdom activity is expressed in judgment and grace. In the New Testament we find that when God is described as working in judgment beyond the church, judgment is clearly linked with grace, issues in grace and has a purpose of grace. Judgment without grace, that is, condemnation does not occur until the final judgment. John describes how light comes into the world and men love darkness rather than light.[19] But this light is not a searchlight of judgment. It is life which brings light to all mankind. It is a sun of righteousness which offers light and life.[20] By

their response men experience it both as a judgment on their
deeds and the source of life. Christ's work outside the church is
therefore a work of grace, and an offer of grace. When men reject that offer, their rebellion is revealed and judgment follows.
But that judgment is still with the purpose of grace.[21]

Paul shows that the purpose of God's judgment in this world
is grace. God's judgment is kindness seeking to lead men to re-
pent.[22] Neither Paul nor John isolates judgment from grace. In
the world outside the church God is at work in Christ through
grace-judgment-grace. It is the light (Christ) which comes into
the world; it is the Spirit of Christ which convicts the world of
sin because they do not believe in him.[23] This theme shows that
we cannot interpret the work of God in the world beyond the
church without relationship to Christ or to the work of grace.
We can look for God at work in grace and judgment, changing
men.

Judgment and grace in society

Can we look for God's judgment and grace in man-in-society,
and not just individual lives? In Romans 10, Paul deals with
God's purpose in the historical process for the Jewish and Gentile nations, considered as social entities rather than as collec-
tions of individuals. The message of grace comes to the Jews.
Those who respond form a remnant; those who reject it grow
deaf and dull of hearing. The nation is judged for its rejection.
But that judgment has a two fold purpose of grace: it is so that
the Gentile nations may be brought in and so that out of envy of
the Gentiles, the Jewish nation may one day accept God's offer.
Here Paul applies the redemptive work of Christ to a group outside the church. In the historical process God is at work in
societies to open them up to receive the full blessings of redemption. Before the nation responds, God acts in its history with the
purpose of grace.

In Romans 13 and 1 Tim. 2 we see grace and judgment at
work in the political structures of society. In Romans 13 the
ruler is under the authority of God. He is to give approval to
what is good, and to be the servant of God to exercize wrath on
the wrongdoer. The purpose of the ruler's authority in society is
that "we may lead a quiet and a peaceable life, godly and res-
pectful in every way. This is good and acceptable in the sight of
God our Saviour, who desires all men to be saved and to come
to the knowledge of the truth."[24] God is at work in the political
structures of society in judgment and grace, to open society up

to the conscious acknowledgement of Christ and thus the fulfilment of the purpose of God for man.

The goal of this work is always to bring men into the kingdom
of God and membership in the body of Christ, in open acceptance of Christ as Lord. We must not identify the action of
God's grace in the world outside the church with the conscious
acknowledgement of the Lordship of Christ by his believing
body, But we do claim that the Lordship of Christ is exercized beyond the church as God acts in judgment and (unacknowledged)
grace, in the world. The difference between unacknowledged
and acknowledged grace lies not in the manner of God's activity,
but in the nature of man's response. Where men respond to
judgment and grace, they receive Christ. Where men do not respond, they incur judgment on themselves. The work of evangelism is therefore to co-operate where God has already been at
work in judgment and grace in his world, on the basis of the victory of Christ applying its effects to man-in-society.

Paul is confident that God works through kings and rulers
and the political structures of society to open society up to the
conscious acknowledgement of Christ, by judgment on its unjust structures and grace in moving it towards God's purpose
for human life. This is the effective operation of the Lordship of
Christ in the world beyond the church, to bring creation to its
God-ordained goal.

This understanding gives a basis for seeing that God is at
work in society beyond the church applying the effects of
Christ's victory in society through social change. Thus all of history becomes the arena where God can be discerned at work,
and all of history is moving towards fulfilment in Christ. We
assert that this is true not only of those activities where Christ
is consciously acknowledged, but also of those areas where
'ground-breaking' is going on, where structures of justice are
being established, where opportunities for choice are being
increased so that people can also choose Christ; here also God's
grace can be seen at work. God's redemption activity is also at
work, even though it is not consciously acknowledged as such.

The image of God

A central purpose of God's kingdom activity is to restore and
recreate man. In explaining redemption in Christ Paul uses
among other categories the category of the restoration of the
image of God in man in Christ. This is linked with his understanding that Christ is the second Adam, the head of a new

humanity. Whether the image of God refers to qualitative aspects of man's humanity, such as his ability to make moral choices, or functional aspects, such as his vice-regency over creation,[25] the Christian community is meant to display some of the marks of restored humanity. Paul clearly thought that the marks of restored humanity included equality between Jews and Gentiles, and an abolition of all distinctions of inferiority based on race, position or sex. The important question is whether some aspects of man's image can be restored for man in the church without a change in the social order. Could God's purpose that there be no distinctions between master and slave be achieved while wider society practised a system of slavery which inevitably affected Christians? If that system of slavery has to be changed, take it ever so long to do so, in order that the image of God may be restored to the new humanity God wills in Christ, must that change not be due in part to the work of Christ? In order that God's purpose for the new humanity in Christ be fulfilled, certain systematic and structural changes have to come in society. These changes are therefore related to what Christ achieved in his cross and resurrection. When non-Christian society beyond the church changes from a slavery system, can we not see also parts of God's image in man being restored, as society is opened up for the full restoration of humanity to be made possible in the church?

The church is always the goal and model for God's purpose for man in society. But to achieve that goal and model, we suggest that the effects of Christ's work in society beyond the church are at work to open society up for the full realization of God's purpose for man in society.

The principalities and powers

God's kingdom activity is cosmic in its scope. Some theologians discern a biblical base for asserting that Christ is at work in society beyond the church to apply the work of redemption in Paul's discussion of the principalities and powers.[26] These powers are, in Paul's thought, demonic forces behind structures in society such as the state and the Jewish religion. Christ triumphed over their rebellion against God on the cross, and is sovereign over them.[27] He is continually disarming them and triumphing over them by overcoming the injustice created by their rebellion in society. This work is not necessarily exercized by the church. Wherever justice replaces injustice in social structures, we can see Christ at work redemptively, as Lord of history.

Some evangelicals suspect that this is an attempt to reduce Pauline teaching about supernatural realities to merely humanistic categories, an attempt to demythologize Paul. However, those evangelicals who espouse a Pauline theology of principalities and powers neither demythologize Paul, nor do they identify structures and demons nor do they deny the reality of personal demons. They ask that a category of Jewish apocalyptic that Paul uses, that of demonic forces behind social realities, be taken in its widest sense, and not limited to demonic personal spirits which possess individuals.

The case for a theology of social change does not rest on the theology of principalities and powers. It rests on Christology. But if this theology of principalities and powers is accepted, it increases our understanding of how Paul thought of Christ as being sovereign of the world.

The groaning of creation

God's kingdom brings the promise of redemption to the whole created order which includes human society. What does Paul refer to when he speaks in Romans 8 of creation groaning as it awaits its final redemption? Some interpreters ask whether the personal categories that Paul uses, such as the bondage to decay and the promise of obtaining the glorious liberty of the children of God, do not point to the fact that Paul was contrasting those who already have the first fruits of the Spirit with the rest of *mankind* (not inanimate creation), who groan as they long for release from bondage into the freedom of God's children.[28] If this case is made, it encourages us to look for signs of God's redemptive work in society which would represent the groaning of mankind as it longs for the fulfilment of this redemption. It longs for its fulfilment because it is aware of the painfulness of bondage to decay and has experienced some aspects of redemption. Christians themselves are not exempt from this groaning, for they experience only the first fruits of redemption and still long for its completion. This theme would then encourage us to look for God at work in society bringing some aspects of redemption on the basis of the work of Christ.

The goal is the church

Taken cumulatively, these themes would encourage us to see the work of struggle for social change and for justice as part of the means of applying the work of redemption which has been won in Christ, whether or not the work is carried on by Christians.

This does not hallow any social change in any direction; it applies only to that social change which would enhance biblical justice in society. The point of the case is that God works towards this goal of enhancing biblical justice in society by other means as well as by conversion and building up the church.

Yet the focus of his work is always the church, and the goal is always the open acknowledgement of Christ and the experience of redeemed humanity in the body of the second Adam. God's redemptive work beyond the church is to open society up both so that that acknowledgement may take place, and so the new humanity may take as complete shape as possible. But his people may not always be his instrument in achieving this goal, and his method may not always be the method of preaching the gospel. For we must ask whether, if the church fails in its task, God is limited to the church. In the Old Testament he raised up Assyria and others to fulfil his purposes, even addressing Cyrus as his servant. The goal of God's action was his people. But the method God used was to alter society in such a way that his purpose for his covenant people could be achieved.

We therefore see from these themes that a biblical case can be made for regarding the work of Christ beyond the church as not fundamentally inferior to his work in the church. Its basis is the same, the victory of Christ on the cross and in his resurrection. Its goal is the same, the creation of a new humanity in Christ which openly acknowledges him as Lord. Its method is complementary to the preaching and teaching ministry of the church: it both opens society up to the possibility of acknowledging that Jesus is Lord, and it enables those who acknowledge his Lordship to experience the full dimensions of the new humanity. We suggest that such a process can be seen in some of the struggles for social change in the Third World, where the weak are seeking full human dignity in struggle with the strong. The strong will also achieve a fuller humanity in true participation with the weak in society. The task of the church in development should be to co-operate with and where possible initiate such a struggle.

Theology, Ideology and Choices in Development

Why do people choose one theology and strategy for development rather than another? Is it solely that some people interpret Scripture faithfully because they set themselves under its authority and others do not? Is it solely because, among those who accept the authority of Scripture, some are more and some are less accurate in their interpretations? Or do people have other commitments which also influence their choice, not only of strategy but also of theology? Do people have values and judgments about how society should be which influence their decisions in these areas?

John F. Robinson clearly thinks that people can be influenced in this way, and that this is a danger to avoid in development thinking. He writes:

Any theology that engages itself with the concerns of the poor and oppressed must deal with complex sociological, economic and political realities. Because of the pluralism in contemporary interpretations of society and the risk that they contain erroneous philosophical assumptions and views of man, evangelicals must be careful not to tie their faith to any particular sociological analysis or theory of change. Theologies of liberation which are yoked to such analyses and theories render themselves highly vulnerable to changing scientific thinking.[29]

Robinson identifies an important point which raises the following questions:

1. Are evangelicals themselves free of a sociological analysis and vision for society?
2. Is it possible for people to have an increasing control over their environment and destiny, without adopting some sociological explanation of the cause of their deprivaton and some theory and programme for change?
3. Is it possible to remain free of a sociological analysis till we adopt one, or do we all unconsciously betray an assumed analysis as soon as we ask the question "Why are poor people poor?"
4. Does loyalty to the authority of Scripture ensure that a person is unbiased in his view of society, or does it give grounds for forming a view on how society should be?
5. Is it possible to engage as Christians in development without having a commitment to some form of world view or ideology, Christian or secular?

We should all recognize that as men living in societies we all reflect the traditions and expectations of our culture. We have to. We all have a world view. David Lim summarizes Charles Kraft's definition of world view in these words:

A world view forms each society's basic model of reality from which the conceptual and behavioural forms (linguistic, social, religious, and technical structure) find their unified meaning. It explains how and why things exist, continue or change, evaluates which forms are proper or improper, gives a psychological stability in times of crisis and provides sociological identity in times of peace. It systematizes and orders the varied perceptions of reality in that society into an overall, integrated perspective.[30]

We adopt the term 'world view' because it is a less loaded term than the word 'ideology'. But ideology is basically the same thing. Philip Wogaman writes:

An ideology is a complex weaving together of values and beliefs. It is our (often unconscious) picture of what society ought to be like. We may believe that this picture describes society as it once was, and therefore we seek to return to that golden age of the past. We may think it describes society as it is, in which case we will stoutly resist all change. Or we may think of it as a vision of what has never been, but may someday be, in which case we shall be 'progressive', or possibly 'revolutionary' . . . All ideologies contain some element of value-judgment — some conception of the good. Hence while all ideology is not the same as religion or philosophy, it may depend on values and beliefs which have religious and philosophical origin.[31]

Evangelicals easily spot world views and ideologies in other theologians who are committed to a Marxist analysis of society and programme for change. Of course Marxists deny that they have an ideology: they claim that they are merely following the scientific laws of history. They are being realistic. But if we say to a Marxist "Why not take the side of the oppressors? It would be more comfortable", he usually resorts to a value-judgment that it is wrong for people to be oppressed. In answering in this way he moves beyond his scientific analysis to give a value-judgment.

Laissez-faire capitalism often claims scientific validity for its vision of society: it claims that it is historically the case that market freedom produces the best economic results. But there is no certainty that capitalism has made its case on economic grounds as the most efficient way to steward resources.[32] Apologists for capitalism usually claim that market freedom preserves the values of individual freedom and initiative. At once they have moved beyond evidence to values, to ideology.

The last twenty years have seen a rejection of both Marxism and capitalism as being doctrinaire systems which blindfold their supporters from seeing the reality of life. In Britain Anthony Wedgewood Benn and Keith Joseph are regarded as equally fanatic and myopic spokesmen for the left and right. What is needed for the complex, difficult problems of the day is simple pragmatism: taking the best solution in the circumstances, judging each case on its own merits. However, as soon as pragmatists say "We have a problem here", be it the problem of poverty or inflation, they cease merely to record reality. They are evaluating reality and saying that according to their value-system poverty is wrong and something should be done about it.

Development agencies all operate with ideology. They have some vision of what society ought to be. This vision informs their strategies and the strategies they support in partner churches and groups in the Third World. It is of the greatest importance that development planners become consciously aware of their ideology, for it greatly affects their work. We give some examples:

a. A highly respected national leader of the Colombian church was reviewing an animal loan project with his North American evangelical colleague. The project is designed to help church families improve their diet and build economic independence; 'starter' animals are given to a few families, and gradually the stewardship/ownership plan is extended to additional families as new animals are born. Yet the Colombian was uneasy.

"We can't do it this way," he finally announced.

"Why not?" asked the startled missionary.

"Because they're making a profit."

"But that's what we want, don't we?"

"No, we are brothers, not capitalists."[33]

b. In South Africa the government in pursuit of its apartheid policies forcibly cleared a city slum of black inhabitants, to force them back to the homelands. They approached the neighbouring Anglican church for help. Had the church supported apartheid, it would not have given them squatting facilities on its compound, which it proceeded to do. The church consciously opposed the ideology of the government.

c. From an historical perspective Carter Lindberg writes:

When we criticize the medieval church for paternalistic attitudes to the poor, as well as an ideology of poverty which posited the spiritual usefulness of the poor to the rich, we should recognize that this is formally similar to our involvement in the ideologies of 'first-world' nations toward 'third-world' nations. In both cases concern to the poor is shaped by an ideology which blinds us to the need for structural changes necessary for redistribution of wealth. E.g., the "help-a-starving-child" approach enables us to avoid serious judgment upon the social reality of poverty and its underlying structural causes.[34]

d. Harvie Conn finds that the policies of evangelical missions and development agencies, far from being neutral in their social engagement, have propagated a sociological viewpoint as uniquely expressive of the Christian faith:

By and large, evangelical missions drew their financial and personal strength from the growing middle class of North America. And from the cultural myths of that class there developed a strong feeling for the identification of Christianity with keynotes of laissez-faire capitalism — individual initiative, fear of governmental control of the market, the power of the consumer in social and economic change, the upward mobility of class structures, democracy as the most suitable (biblical) form of government, organization as the key to maximum development, the inevitability of progress, the middle class as the source of change and progress in every society. Pietism's highly individual mood, its ameliorative focus on societal change, its emphasis on the self-discipline of the virtues of moderation, thrift, hard work, only served to reinforce these cultural patterns of understanding and sanction the cultural myths, without any fully biblical evaluation of their legitimacy and value.[35]

In short we echo the call of Bishop German Schmitz at the recent Conference of Bishops in Latin America. "Let him who is without ideology cast the first stone."[36]

Once we have recognized our ideology, it is vital to evaluate it by biblical criteria. We need to work at producing biblical criteria for a just society which are acceptable to the east and west, that is criteria which do not presume that any one way of reading the Bible or organizing society is ideologically pure or objective. The grammatico-historical method of reading the Bible is in fact informed by Graeco-Roman tenets of literary criticism; look at the trouble we have with Paul's use of the Old Testament.[37] In organizing society we have seen in our overview of the literature that some theologies of development take over other ideologies wholesale and evaluate the Bible in terms of those ideologies.

Evangelicals need to develop biblical criteria for society around three foci: the transcendent Spirit of God who is not bound to any situation, who transforms every situation and enables us to be freed from the shackles of our own world views and ideologies; the community of the Spirit through whom the power of God is manifest to redeem what the power of man distorts, by reconciliation, forgiveness and sharing; and the Word of the Spirit which always challenges the community to fresh evaluation of their obedience.

It is absolutely vital that such criteria be developed in a multi-cultural debate. We can be exposed to our own blindspots in reading the Bible not so much by continuing to read the Bible in our own context, or listening to scholars from our own context, but by listening to those who read the Bible in other contexts. A Christian from South Africa told one of us that he came to see the wrongs of apartheid only when he came and studied with Christians in England. Therefore we must give those evangelicals who profess loyalty to Scripture the benefit of the doubt when we hear them interpreting the Scriptures in a way that lies outside our own cultural evangelical traditions.[38]

Theology, Strategy and Development Agencies

For evangelicals the debate focuses on the issues of a theology of social change versus a theology of social preservation, and on a strategy of non-violent struggle versus modernization. What are the implications for evangelical development agencies and national churches?

Theology

It is vitally necessary to be clear about the difference between theology and ideology, and the effect they have on each other. Evangelicals in India produced the Madras Declaration on Evangelical Social Action in 1979. They called for the churches "to assess critically the role of Christian institutions for education, health, agriculture and relief, according to the principles of people's participation, justice and service to the poorest" . . . "to refuse to co-operate with structures and laws which in our opinion promote injustice," and "to be the agent of the Kingdom in society to create social structures which preserve and promote human rights and establish peace and dignity." A number of critical responses were received, including one which noted: "There is nothing particularly Christian about these recommendations. The unique possibilities of social action based on local churches and assemblies are bypassed."[39]

Is this criticism a theological criticism? No. It is a criticism of the strategy on the grounds that it is not distinctively Christian. We hope our paper shows the pitfalls to be avoided before we can claim that a strategy is distinctively Christian. The question should be whether any strategy has a sufficiently Christian theological basis, apart from whether or not only Christians practise it. For a strategy to be operated or based on churches does not guarantee that it is Christian.

The critic admitted in discussion that he did not fault the theology of the statement. If that is the case then some other values have prevented his seeing the place of structural social change in Christian action. Has a different ideology informed his judgment and prevented his seeing the implications of the theological statements of the Declaration?

The details of the case are not important but the event is. It illustrates clearly what will happen in the evangelical constituency as evangelicals develop theologies and strategies of social change. Some will react to the strategies for ideological reasons and identify the issues as theological.

This will create unnecessary divisions. Western church leaders and development agency boards should clearly differentiate in their own minds and in their literature between theology and ideology in order to preserve evangelical fellowship. This does not mean that theology will have no effect on ideology, but it does mean that we must be clear about what we disagree on. People may disagree with Ron Sider about the causes of disparity in economic wealth, as Michael Alison does.[40] It is confused thinking to disagree with him for this reason and at the same time base an attack on his work on selective use of Scripture and careless exegesis.

Others will read evangelical theologies and strategies, and because they may fail to find traditional evangelical terminology, or find it used in new ways to cover a wider field of vision, they will again suspect that a fundamental theological mistake is being made. For example, those who are attempting to understand Paul's theology of principalities and powers over a wider canvas are thought to be abandoning the identification of these powers with demonic forces.[41] Or evangelicals who come to the Scriptures with the questions raised by liberation theologians are suspect unless they explicitly affirm the acceptance of the traditional understanding of the doctrines of the cross and resurrection and the Holy Spirit in individual categories.[42] Both evangelical gadflies and watchdogs are necessary.[43] But they must not be distrustful of each other. They must both in good faith return to the Scriptures as their groundwork and ultimate bar of authority.

Strategy

It is important to develop strategies which produce true development in each socio-economic context. Some evangelicals are clearly searching for strategies which encourage the struggle of the poor to attain human dignity. They are aware that unless a positive strategy is developed along these lines, pragmatic strategies will both reflect the interests of the donor culture and play into the hands of those who benefit from the current system.

Partnership

If the issue is the relationship between the strong and the weak and how both can grow to equality, then the partnership between western churches and agencies and national bodies in the Third World should model a pattern for that growth.[44]

Ecclesiology

If the goal of all Christian development is to open society up for the acknowledgement of Jesus as Lord by a redeemed humanity, then it is vital that local churches are involved in development work at every stage. Western agencies should reflect on the implications of any proposal to bypass national and local churches in the Third World.

Evangelical affirmation

At the heart of the theology we propose for social change is the atonement, the resurrection and the work of the Holy Spirit.

The cross and resurrection of Jesus spelt the decisive defeat of evil, took the consequences of man's rebellion, and made possible man's entrance to the kingdom of God and the formation of a new humanity on earth. The cross and resurrection define the nature and purpose of God's work in and beyond the church through the Spirit of God on the basis of the work of Christ. God's work beyond the church and his work in the church are complementary. Beyond the church he is working in society to open society up to acknowledge Jesus as Lord and to make possible that new humanity which is being formed in the church. In the church the Spirit is building new relationships of love and justice which model to society the nature of God's plan for man, both as judgment on society and hope for it.[45]

(We wish to record our gratitude to the following for their assistance in making books available: Partnership in Mission, Philadelphia; the Library of the United Theological College, Bangalore; the Documentation Centre of the Indian Social Institute, Bangalore; and to Professor Lindberg of the Institute for Ecumenical Research, Strasbourg, for making his unpublished paper available to us.

We are also grateful to members of the World Evangelical Fellowship Conference on Theology of Development in London in March 1980. Their valuable discussion of our paper enabled us to correct and clarify a number of points. We are particularly grateful to Rev. Andrew Kirk who gave the formal response to our paper, and to Rev. Dr. Chris Wigglesworth for their suggestions for detailed improvements.)

CHAPTER FOUR

Development: Its Secular Past and its Uncertain Future

Development: Its Secular Past and its Uncertain Future

TOM SINE

When it initiated its first consultation on a theology of development, the World Evangelical Fellowship embarked on an historic journey. In preparation for this important journey it is essential to: 1) analyze the essentially secular origin and values of western development; and 2) anticipate the challenges of an uncertain future that are likely to confront development specialists in the eighties and beyond.

The Secular Origin of Western Development

Before we attempt to articulate a Christian Theology of Development we must understand the essentially secular 'Theology' of contemporary development, its origins and implicit values. Only then can we begin to give expression to a statement that reflects a uniquely divergent biblical perspective. In order to surface these implicit values the following questions will be asked of western development. What are the implicit images of: 1. The Better Future? 2. God and His Universe? 3. Nature of Persons? 4. The Pathway to the Achievement of that Better Future?

I. What is the implicit view of the better future in Western development?

Western development is a child of the European and American Enlightenment. It is based on the implicit belief that human society is inevitably progressing toward the attainment of a temporal, materialistic kingdom. In fact, the certain belief that unending economic and social progress is a natural condition of free persons has become the secular religion of the west.

Somehow the millenial expectation of the inbreaking of a new transcendent kingdom was temporalized and secularized into the expectation of a future of unlimited economic and techno- logical growth. In Francis Bacon's book *The New Atlantis* we are shown the first vision in western history of a technological paradise achieved solely through human instrumentality.

Implicit in this progressive view of the future was the firm conviction that economic progress would automatically result in social and moral progress. Here then is a view of the better future that is primarily economic focusing largely on human activities of production and consumption. Not surprisingly the 'good life' became synonymous with self-seeking and one's ability to produce and consume goods and services.

The expansive nature of the Western dream of progress moti- vated westerners to go beyond their own national boundaries in search of both resources and markets as the Industrial Revo- lution began. The realization of the American dream was made possible by the appropriation of enormous areas of land and the resources they obtained from native Americans. The great leap forward of industrial and economic growth in the west would not have been possible without the abundant relatively inexpen- sive resources acquired through colonization of countries in the southern hemisphere.

One of the realities that Christians must grasp is that "mis- sionary activity has gone hand in hand with colonization for almost two millenia. No matter how we interpret the underlying relations between the two orders, it is self-evident that political expansion and the church's expansion in the world have covered the same ground, geographically and chronologically."[1]

Since the church's expansion went hand in hand with western economic and political expansion the question with which we must struggle is: To what extent have the values of secular western development permeated Christian development?

Interestingly, Marxist ideology was born out of the same Western ferment and also sees society moving towards a tem- poral future that is singularly economic and political. Its inten- tion is to ensure that all peoples participate in this future and Marxists believe in its inevitability.

As we enter the eighties virtually no one any longer believes in the inevitability of economic, technological and social progress other than Marxists. The events of the seventies have sounded the death knell for the enlightened belief that humankind could achieve a utopia here on earth. In spite of this new sobering awareness the essential image of the better future implicit in contemporary development has not significantly changed since the beginnings of western expansion. At the very core of contemporary development is a notion that the better future is synonymous with economic growth. The 'better life' of persons is really defined principally in economic terms. Nations which have experienced major economic and technological growth are described as 'developed'; those which haven't are characterized as 'underdeveloped'. In spite of the growing awareness of the negative human and environmental consequences of unrestrained growth, the 'developed' world has become a showcase of the 'ideal' future for the 'underdeveloped' world. The apparent superiority of the 'developed' image of the ideal future has directly influenced the definition and goals of contemporary development. Thirty years ago the primary goal of western development in the Third World was 'maximization of GNP per capita'. Today the goal has been broadened to focus increasingly on 'basic needs' to raise the economic level of the world's poorest people.[2]

John Sommers argues that "it has become increasingly clear that economic well-being is not a sufficient goal and the measuring of development on the materialistic basis of per capita gross national product is inadequate and often misleading."[3] He goes on to advocate that development should be defined in spiritual and cultural terms as well as economic. There are some nonwestern models that are based on a broader understanding of the scope of development.

For example, Gandhi had a very different vision for the future of his people from the one that is implicit in the western model. "The Mahatma was wholly opposed to those who argued that India's future lay in imitating the industrial technological society of the west. India's salvation he argued lay in 'unlearning what she has learned in the past 50 years'. He challenged almost all of the western ideals that had taken root in India. Science should not order human values he argued, technology should not order society, and civilization was not the indefinite multiplication of human wants, but their limitation so that essentials could be shared by all."[4]

Gandhi's image of the better future for India was a nation of 600,000 decentralized villages which were highly self-sufficient units in which traditional culture, religion and family life were strengthened. While longing to see grinding poverty ended, he opposed development which would create material affluence, because he was convinced that affluence would lead to cultural erosion and moral bankruptcy. His vision for the future gave primacy not to economic developmnent, but the development of the inner spirit and the reinforcement of positive values within traditional culture.

As this consulation begins to struggle to articulate a uniquely biblical perspective on development we must ask ourselves:

A. To what extent is the image of the better future implicit in contemporary Christian development simply a reflection of the western images of economic and technological growth, materialism, consumerism and individualism?

B. To what extent should our images of the better future focus on the development of spiritual life, human relations and the reinforcement of traditional cultural values?

C. Should the images of the better future that motivate Christian development activity be derived from western culture, Marxist ideology, the host culture, the church or biblical sources?

D. What is a biblical image of God's intended future for all peoples and how should that be incorporated in Christian development planning within different cultures?

II. What is the implicit view of God and his universe in Western development?

Western views of development are tied not only to singularly secular notions of the better future, but also to secular views of God and his universe that have their origins in the Enlightenment. In sixteenth century England Francis Bacon drew an historic line between the 'words of God' and the 'works of God'. By that act he gave major momentum towards a new dualistic view of the universe. Essentially all in the natural order that can be experienced through the senses was lumped into the 'works of God'. The revelational and spiritual aspects of existence were pigeon-holed under the 'words of God'.

As a direct consequence of this dualism, not only God but all sense of divine intention and sacred mystery were forcibly evicted from the natural world. Much of western culture was left with a empty meaningless universe freed from any divine presence or purpose. The Enlightenment had encouraged this scientific secularization of the universe insisting as Bacon had, that it is a realm that can best be understood through empirical science not divine revelation. For many, if God existed at all he existed outside the natural universe, impotent, passive and unable to intervene in his world.

Not only was the Creator seen as passive but his creation was also seen as a passive realm, a grab bag of physical resources available for the taking. This dualistic view of God and his universe has resulted in a desacralization of his creation. Westerners learned to think of the world around them as nothing but resources to be exploited to enable them to achieve their materialistic dreams for the future, as Jeremy Rifkin explains: "Faith in the liberating power of materialism carries with it one critical assumption, the belief the earth possesses unlimited abundance. The formulators of liberalism, the men of the Age of Reason and the Enlightenment, had no doubt that the earth would yield more wealth than could possibly be used . . . In the 1600's the new world, the greatest frontier known, was just opening up for exploitation. By the beginning of the next century, industrialism had begun. Wherever people looked it seemed that the world held more — more wealth, more prosperity, more productivity, more knowledge to be used in the service of humanity. The obvious contrast with the unchanging order of the Middle Ages was proof to all persons of reason that the new age was superior to all that had come before.''[5] This secularized view of God and his universe was foundational to the economic growth and expansion of an age of western development. Marxism has, of course, explicitly repudiated the existence and activity of God in his world.

The dualism of Bacon and his followers has borne its fruit in our age. In contemporary development as in much of western culture there is no belief that God lives and acts in history. The world and its future are perceived to be solely in the hands of man. Contemporary development theory is premised on a thorough-going secularization of the natural and human orders. Contemporary development literature gives not the slightest consideration to the possibility that God is, or that he has any influence on human affairs. In fact, the literature tends to deny even the existence of any realm beyond human sensory experience. It is assumed in development theory that 'developed' people have the responsibility, through rational development planning, to enable as many of the world's 'underdeveloped' people as possible to join the inner circle of economic growth and prosperity. Neither God nor any other spiritual forces are seen as active in the process of development.

The dualism that evicted God not only from his world but from existence itself has also contributed to the work of desacralization of God's world. The massive exploitation of global resources has brought us to a new reality. The *First Report to the Club of Rome* in 1973 called to everyone's attention the reality that the earth is not infinite, it is finite. This reality more than any other contemporary insight has put to rest the western belief in both the inevitability and indeed the possibility of all people fully participating in the western dream.

Far from being simply a passive malleable resource as Bacon had suggested, we have recently discovered that for every act we take against God's world it seems to have a capability to counter punch. We can no longer thoughtlessly exploit the natural order. We are being forced to consider the consequence of every act we take. We are being forced to perceive ourselves as stewards not of passive resources but of a vast, active fragile planetary system. Recent development literature is beginning belatedly to reflect this new view. Unfortunately transnational corporations are slower to espouse this new awareness.

In the discussing of a biblical theology of development we need to answer the following questions:

A. To what extent have assumptions regarding God that are implicit in western development permeated Christian development? For example, do Christian development activities tend to reflect a view of God: 1) as an active initiator and participant? 2) as a passive endorser and encourager of human initiative? 3) as essentially outside Christian development activities (but active in church evangelistic and church-planting activities)?

B. To what extent have assumptions regarding the nature of God's world that are implicit in western development permeated Christian development? For example, do Christian development activities tend to reflect a view of the nature of the world: 1) as a uniquely sacred realm, filled with God's presence and directed by his purposes, entrusted to the responsible stewardship of humankind? 2) as an exclusively material realm that is finite and fragile that must be responsibly stewarded? 3) as a source of passive abundant material resources to be fully exploited to achieve maximum economic growth?

C. What is a biblical image of the role and initiative of God in human history generally and development planning specifically?

D. What is a biblical image of the nature of God's world and humankind's relationship to that world?

III. What is the implicit view of persons in Western development?

Closely related to the image of God and his universe implicit in western development is the image of humanity. When Francis Bacon divided the natural and the sacred realm he unwittingly divided body from soul. Even as the universe was reduced to nothing but the sum of its physical properties, so many in the west learned to view persons as nothing but the sum of their biological components. In a universe freed from divine presence and purpose, human beings were increasingly seen as alone. Their lives were seen as having no sense of divine intention or innate worth.

In an essentially economic world-view their worth was seen as largely derivative. To the extent that the individual contributed to the collective economic growth, to that extent the individual was viewed as having worth. Therefore one of the primary characteristics of persons in western culture is to identify themselves with and indeed derive significance and meaning for life from their ability to produce and consume.

Self-interest and self-seeking became the basis of this new society of economic progress and growth. It was widely assumed during the Enlightenment that if individuals pursued their own private self-interest it would work for the common good. John Locke was the archapostle of this new doctrine. He condemned the American Indians for living on land filled with abundant resources and not exploiting them in order to live lives of personal affluence.

"With Locke, the fate of modern man and women is sealed. From the time of the Enlightenment on, the individual is reduced to the hedonistic activity of production and consumption to find meaning and purpose. People's needs and aspirations, their dreams and desires, all become confined to the pursuit of material self-interest."[6]

In our age even as God and his world have come to be understood in the starkest secular terms in contemporary development, so has human nature. Momentum begun in the Enlightenment has reduced man to nothing but the sum of his biological core and his behavioural surface. Since the world has no overarching purpose or divine presence, neither does the contemporary individual.

His sense of meaning, identity and worth are derived from his ability to participate and compete successfully in an essentially economic world. Increasingly Americans have learned to derive their very identity from what they produce and what they consume. Those in western culture not able to participate fully in the economic rat race are seen as a threat to the entire system. Persons are reduced to their economic value to the large technocratic order. Pope John Paul has declared that capitalism reduces persons to consuming things and communism reduces them to economic things.

The seventies have accurately been characterized as the 'me first' decade in America. The self seeking encouraged by Locke and Jefferson has in contemporary western culture become an absolute mania. The good life for the individual is strongly oriented towards acquisitive, consumptive and status-seeking behaviour even among Christians.

Modern development conceiving this world as primarily an economic realm tends to talk about human personality, human activity and human goals in largely economic terms such a human resources, beneficiaries, etc. Therefore, modern development activity tends to foster a reductionistic view of human personality and activity.

A. To what extent have assumptions regarding human nature that are implicit in contemporary development permeated Christian development? for example,

   1. Do Christian development activities reflect a view of persons as nothing but the sum of their biological endowments, their social behaviour and their economic activity?

   2. Do Christian development activities reflect the goals for personal life principally in the areas of economic initiative, getting ahead materially and moving up the status ladder?

   3. Do Christian development agencies unconsciously reflect an affirmation of personal worth derived from a person's economic production, his acquisitive success and his upward mobility?

   4. Do Christian development specialists reflect lifestyles that are highly involved with acquisitive, materialistic status-seeking values of the secular society?

B. What is a distinctly biblical view of human personality? of human worth? of the goals for human life in relation to God's intended future? of God's role in enabling persons to attain those goals? should we participate in development with both Christians and non-Christians?

IV. What is the implicit view of the pathway to this better future in Western development?

Even though the proponents of western progress believed in the inevitability of the attainment of a materialistic paradise on earth, they also believed it would be achieved only through the initiative of rational man. The instrumentality of man not the initiative of God was essential to create this new age.

Bacon proclaimed that he had discovered a new promethean power that would enable humankind to fashion a new technological utopia. That power was the rational human ability to examine empirically the natural world. Empirically derived knowledge was the new power that would enable humankind to subdue a passive nature and create a new materialistic utopia.

Locke, believing that all human activity is based on materialistic self-interest, encouraged self seeking as yet another means to achieve this enlightened paradise. Thomas Jefferson incorporated in the 'Religion of America' the Lockean life goal of the individualistic pursuit of happiness as a cardinal doctrine.

Adam Smith, following on the philosophy of Locke, created a new economics of growth that became an essential pathway to the goal of temporal progress. He removed any sense of morality from economics. Essentially he postulated that individuals should have complete freedom to pursue self-interest in the quest for economic gain. He maintained that if they were given that freedom the invisible hand of natural law would ensure that the common good would be achieved through private selfishness. This is the premise of capitalism.

"Smith championed the cause of a growing class of manufacturers who saw their interests stifled by government monopolies and the closed ranks of the mercantilists. Just as Locke had promoted the social interests of bourgeois merchants and traders, Smith appealed to 'natural laws' based on Newtonian-Baconian science to legitimatize the economic interests of the new industrial entrepreneurs."[7]

Since contemporary advocates of development no longer view progress as inevitable and since there is no God even to lend endorsement, even greater responsibility has been shifted to human initiative to set the world right. Until recently it was believed that global development could best be achieved through the intervention of high technology and advanced science. With the publication of Schumacher's classic *Small is Beautiful* in 1973, people began to shift their attention to smaller and more appropriate technological responses to development needs in the Third World. Science and technology, however, are still seen as a primary pathway to the better future. All that has changed is the realization of the importance of appropriate application whether we are talking about community health, sanitation or agriculture.

The laissez-faire economics introduced by Adam Smith is still

alive and well and provides the foundation for most contemporary development planning. This doctrine, based on a belief that
private selfishness will secure the common good has, however,
been strenuously challenged in many countries. During the past
70 years a host of socialist regimes have sought to demonstrate
another pathway of planned economics that elevates the common good above private gain. Marxist ideology opposes western
economics and development planning as obscuring the real
problem of the overthrow and replacement of unjust structures.

More recently the disastrous environmental and human consequences of global corporate expansion has seriously challenged the premise of Adam Smith's economic model causing
many to call for a new economic order. Even so most western
development activity tends to accept this idea of economic
growth as given and it is seen as a primary means, in its diverse
expressions, to a better economic future.

As long as the better collective and personal future is defined
almost exclusively in economic and physical terms, contemporary development has no pathway to that future other than the
appropriate application of science and technology, growth
economics and utilitarian education.

A. To what extent have the assumptions regarding the pathway
   to the better future implicit in contemporary development
   activity permeated Christian development?
   1. To what extent have Christian agencies become depen-
      dent on western science, technology, economics and
      education to promote a better future for persons in the
      Third World?
   2. When a Christian agency leaves a successful project in a
      Third World country, are the people more dependent on
      western science, technology and economics or on God?
B. In light of the broader biblical image of the future that we
   seek for all people, what are some other divergent pathways
   Christian agencies could use to pursue those futures?
C. Given a biblical understanding of God's intentions for the
   human future, how should Christian development agencies
   seek to relate their activity to the larger mission of the
   church in the world?

Development: An Uncertain Future

To articulate effectively a biblical theology of development we
must not only understand its secular origins, we must also anticipate its uncertain future. Every indicator seems to suggest

that the final two decades of the 20th century are going to be filled with dramatic change that will have its greatest impact on the planetary poor. The eighties will be the decade of the poor.

By 1955 virtually all Third World countries secured their political independence from the colonial systems of the past. Between 1955 and 1975 this planet experienced the greatest period of economic growth in the history of civilization. During this unprecedented period of economic growth the gap between rich and poor nations widened at a dramatic rate. This growing inequity motivated the 'Group of 77' (now comprising more than 100 Third World countries) to make a presentation in the United Nations in 1974 calling for a New International Economic Order. While the nations of the north have, somewhat reluctantly, consented to discuss their proposals for a more just international economic order, they have not been willing to adopt any significant reforms in the present system. Therefore, it can be reasonably expected in light of this resistance that as the northern hemisphere continues to pursue a course of maximum economic growth, much of that growth will come at the expense of the southern hemisphere. And the gap between rich and poor will continue to expand through the eighties.[8]

This relentless commitment by the west to unrestrained economic growth and the projected growth of global population to six billion persons by the year 2000 puts our planet under mounting stress. The U.S. Office of Technology Assessment predicts that the projected levels of combined economic and population growth will seriously threaten the carrying capability of our finite plant through massive pollution of air and water, deforestation, creation of deserts, elimination of natural areas of wildlife habitats, depletion of fish stocks, progressive simplification and homogenization of nature. They conclude that these pressures on the environmental system will contribute to at least double digit inflation world wide for the foreseeable future. Of course those who will be most dramatically impacted by high inflation will be the poor.[9]

To compound this situation further many transnational corporations are consciously involved with altering customs and tastes of persons within Third World culture. Their intention is to redefine the nature of the good life for persons in all cultures in order to expand the global market for Coke, Twinkies, Nabisco crackers and a host of other western consumer products. This transnational economic activity is expedited by the growing control of a broad range of communication networks and technologies by transnational corporations. A 'communication in-

dustrial complex' is being formed which controls everything
from satellite communications systems to a growing number of
television and media networks within Third World nations.[10]
The consequences of this conscious effort to change culture for
the sake of market expansion and the use of media to expedite
this process are likely to foster widespread cultural destabil-
ization and westernization throughout the southern hemisphere
in the future.

Beyond cultural imposition "global corporations exploit their
"perior bargaining power in weak disorganized societies to
ᴖrry out a series of activities which can offer exceptionally high
profits for the world-wide enterprise, but which often promote
economic and social backwardness within countries: the manipulation of transfer prices rob the countries of foreign exchange
and reasonable earnings from exports. The technology transfer-
red by multinationals, which is usually designed for the home
market in a developed society, is inappropriate to the needs of
poor countries. It often displaces jobs and is overpriced. The
products manufactured in poor countries are beyond the reach
of the majority of people who lack the money to buy them.
Such products are consumed by local élites in enclaves of affluence or they are exported. The export-led model of development
of which the multinational corporation has been the major
engine has meant crippling debt and increasing dependence on
rich countries, their private banks and the international lending
agencies which they control. Because of their superior control
over capital, technology, and marketing, global corporations
can dominate local economics and pre-empt the power to plan
for the society."[11] Therefore as multinationals increase in their
influence and power in the economic life of the southern hemisphere they will also increase their control over the societies in
which they do business.

Not only are the poorer people of this planet likely to lose in
the competition for economic resources; they are also likely to
be compromised by increasing competition for arable land. As
we approach six billion people on our small spaceship, the land
on which we grow food is dramatically shrinking. In the United
States and Western Europe thousands of acres of prime agricul-
tural land are lost every year to parking lots, freeways, suburban sprawl and urban development. In the Third World
desertification, deforestation and urban expansion are also
devouring large quantitites of land that had been used to produce food and fuel. The consequence of this situation is that the
affluent western consumer is increasingly competing with his

neighbour in the southern hemisphere for food grown on his land. This has resulted in land in Guatemala, Haiti and Costa Rica being taken out of domestic food production to provide Americans with between meal snacks. Evidence indicates that increased beef exports from Central America to the United States have contributed to the growth of malnutrition and hunger in those regions.[12]

The issue of the just use of arable land is likely to become a major focus of discussion in the eights as the problems of hunger and the dependency of the global poor on imported food both increase. Michael Harrington in his book *The Vast Majority* states that there are 70 million people in imminent danger of starvation, 400 million who are chronically malnourished and fully one billion who don't get enough to eat. Forecasts suggest that the number of hungry people in the world will more than double by 1995. Add to this reality the fact that the poor nations are becoming increasingly dependent upon imports of food staples. The countries of South Asia, for example, which imported five to six per cent of their food in 1960 and eight to nine per cent in 1975 will need to import 17-18 per cent of their food by 1995 if historical trends continue.[13]

Given the energy inputs required to produce those staples in the west and escalating cost of that energy, it is altogether possible that countries will not be able to afford to purchase the food they will need to offset their growing domestic deficits in the future. What we are belatedly discovering as population continues to explode is that the earth's resources are not infinite. They are finite. Increasing competition for land, food, energy and minerals will continue to benefit the world's wealthy at the expense of the world's poor.

Perhaps no other area of population growth is going to place greater stress on human and environmental systems in the eighties and nineties than the overwhelming growth of Third World cities. "By the end of the century three quarters of all Latin Americans and one third of all Asians and Africans will . . . be living in cities."[14] Mexico City is projected to become the world's largest city growing from its present population of 11 million to more than 31 million persons by the year 2000. Sao Paulo, Brazil is forecast to be second in size with 25 million.[15] The extent of peril for persons in these areas of urban explosion can scarcely be exaggerated. These populations are expanding with virtually no comparable expansion in basic life support systems in food, water, sanitation and housing.

One cannot look at the planetary future without considering

the political, spiritual and social dimensions of societal change. These are much harder to predict, but still merit discussion. In the political realm, the dramatic expansion of global arms expenditures from $350 billion in 1976 to $425 billion in 1979 has significantly increased the danger of conflict while using vast planetary resources that could be sued for human development. The widespread availability of nuclear and other megadeath weapon systems will also increase the risk of their use.[16] Some futurists believe that the possibilities of polarization between the northern and southern hemispheres is even greater than the present chill between east and west.

At any point in history the principalities and powers are in a life and death struggle with the forces of light. Human society generallly and the Church specifically is going to be faced with an avalanche of human problems, rising deprivation and threatened persecution. In addition there are going to be significant changes within the Church. For example, Buhlmann predicts in his book, *The Coming of the Third Church,* that over half the Christians in the world are going to be living in the southern hemisphere by the year 2000. This new reality was influential in the Pope's recent decision to visit Latin America. It means that the centre of power of the Church is likely to shift from the northern to the southern hemisphere. Western development agencies need to come to grips with this shift and re-examine their relationship with the Church in the southern hemisphere. In view of growing global inequity there will probably be an increasing struggle between those who see the Gospel in largely personal terms and those who see it primarily in terms of liberation from unjust economic and political structures.

The growing political conservatism of the west, double digit inflation and the erosion of the discretionary income among contributors in western nations are likely to combine to reduce the amount of money available for development. If Christian organizations don't design intentional systems of co-operation we are likely to see a decade of increasing competition for a shrinking financial resource.

How should the people of God generally and Christian development agencies specifically respond to the anticipated challenges of the next two decades? Should we give up on the poor? The future? The mission of the Church? Thousands of American Christians caught up in an eschatology of escape have done just that. In view of their eschatology they genuinely believe that they can't make any difference in their world. They hold absolutely no hope for the future other than their own personal escape. This great escape mentality in reality becomes an incredible cop-out from all that God calls us to be and to do. Believing the human future to be hopeless they often subscribe to the secular religion of the west using their resources to get a piece of the corporate consumer pie while the getting is still good. The consequence of this latter-day fatalism and consumptive lifestyle is devastating to the mission of Christ's Church. Incredible quantities of resources that could be used in the mission of the Church in development, evangelism and church planting are squandered in the pursuit of a different dream.

Instead of allowing the anticipated challenges of the next two decades to immobilize us into a non-biblical fatalism, we need to see them as opportunities to be the People of God in a way we have never been before. Frankly, a 'business as usual' approach in our Christian organizations and churches will not begin to impact the human challenges facing us in the future. Only a new radical biblical offensive, beginning in our own lives, churches and organizations, has the possibility of effectively responding to these kinds of challenges. Christian development agencies need to increase dramatically their capability to respond to the anticipated needs of the eighties before these become critical.

Therefore, I propose that we:
1. Develop an ongoing capability to anticipate new areas of human deprivation and crisis before they arrive in order that we may have time to mobilize resources and design development responses.
2. Draft a biblical theology of development that will enable us to respond more passionately and aggressively to the anticipated challenges of the future, striving to achieve God's intended future for all peoples.
3. Redesign all our agency development activities so that they are fully congruent with our biblical theology — to include everything from our approach to health care to servanthood management models.
4. Create a process to design co-operatively a broad spectrum of imaginative new biblical responses to the anticipated challenges of the eighties and nineties in areas such as economic development, multinational accountability, cultural development, etc.
5. Establish new co-operative relationships between Christian agencies to reduce competition, duplication and use more effectively God's resources to expand into new areas of human need, in order to develop a global strategy to address co-operatively the escalating deprivation of the eighties.

6. Challenge believers and Christian organizations in the west
    to promote the just use of global resources through seeking
    to simplify dramatically personal and institutional lifestyles
    to free more resources of time, gifts and money for the work
    of God's kingdom among the poor.
7. Commit western development agencies and their staff to
    lead the western Church into patterns of voluntary simpli-
    city through:
    a. Dramatically reducing overheads by decorating offices
       simply, exclusively using budget hotels, restaurants and
       transportation, significantly increasing the use of volun-
       teers at all levels and seeking to reduce all overhead that
       isn't absolutely essential to mission;
    b. Seeking separate funding for all agency overhead expen-
       ses so that the full amount of contributed dollars can be
       directly used in Third World development;
    c. Making a commitment to a lifestyle of voluntary simpli-
       city a condition of employment (leaving it to the indi-
       vidual to find God's direction as to how to pursue simpli-
       city in his own life);
    d. Providing regular seminars, within agencies on biblical
       discipleship, Third World mission and voluntary sim-
       plicity.
8. Use the resources that are made available through voluntary
    simplicity and cooperation to increase significantly our
    ability to respond to those anticipated areas of greatest
    urban and rural needs in the eighties.

In view of the anticipated human needs of the next two
decades, Christian development agencies need to take the initiative in challenging the church to mobilize all of its resources
and creativity to increase significantly its capacity for global
mission. We have absolutely no idea of the change God could
bring in a world of escalating need if we were to commit ourselves fully and our resources to seeking first his kingdom of
justice, righteousness, reconciliation, peace and love in antici-
pation of that day when it fully comes.

CHAPTER FIVE

The Implications of Western
Theologies of Development for
Third World Countries and Churches

5

The Implications of Western Theologies of Development for Third World Countries and Churches

M. R. MATHEWS

Since the Lausanne Congress in 1974, many Evangelicals have come to realize that both physical welfare and spiritual salvation are partners in the development of the whole person. We are also coming to realize that we need to evolve a concept of development which gives a sense of equality and dignity. Economic growth is of course necessary. Without it, social justice can become the equal sharing of abject squalor. But it is not sufficient. We must also be concerned for quality of life as a whole. To this end we are keen to develop self-reliance along with justice and economic growth.

Do Western secular development programmes encourage self-reliance, equality and dignity in their partners in Third World countries? I perceive some underlying assumptions in their programmes.

a. Western developed (and Christianized) countries have more knowledge and skill than Third World countries. So they can recommend programmes and patterns for development with some confidence. If Third World countries follow these patterns closely, their days of needing aid will be numbered.

b. Western influence through consumerism and cosmopolitan secular values will break down age-old cultural hindrances to development.

c. Simple mathematics show that if there were fewer people in the Third World, their resources would go further. Reduction of population through birth control or birth spacing would automatically promote development.

Broadly speaking, it seems that Western programmes of development have the following aims in Third World countries:

To extend life expectancy, to increase per capita consumption of protein and calories, to give primary and secondary education, to give vocational training, to impart skills, to provide better accommodation, to immunize against diseases and to develop health and sanitary services.

In recent years a number of thinkers and strategists in the West have become more hesitant about advocating such measures. They see a number of evils inherit in modernization. These evils may be present, but to us in the Third World it sounds as if the West is pulling the ladder of development up after them. For example, some urge that small is beautiful, but this seems to imply that developing countries should not invest in the large scale industrialization which has given the West such advantages, and that they should freeze their present levels of development. Others advocate the virtues of simplicity and appropriate technology. This sounds like a justification for leaving us with an inferior technology. While the developed world as a whole bids everyone remember that there is an energy crisis, they seem to forget that the developed world consumes 95% of the total energy used in the world. So as the West argues that development brings pollutions, delinquency, drug abuse and family problems in its wake, it advises that the Third World learn from its experience, and forego the path to development. This sounds too much like advice to continue to remain poor.

There is a very clear interrelationship between the economies of the West and the economies of Third World countries. First World countries owe their affluence by and large to the colonial era when they were able to extract the basic raw materials with which to set up their major industries from those countries which are now the Third World. The rise in commodity prices during the seventies, especially in oil, has slowed down their rate of growth to some extent. But it seems to me that the role of Third World countries is still to produce second class citizens, second class prefabricated goods and second class products with intermediate degrees of second class technology. They are politically and socio-economically oppressed, marginalized and despised.

I would wish us to stop and look at the problem from within the Third World itself. Come to my land of India. We are looking again at the real causes of poverty, we are examining the psychology of poor people. It is not possible any longer to find simple answers in population control, increased food production and more employment. Consider these problems in our villages. A labourer who cannot be certain of his wages cannot be made to reinvolve his money or work on buildings, modernized farming, soil conservation or improved irrigation drainage. A farmer who knows that a significant proportion of his crops will be taken by the landlord or eaten by rats has little incentive to improve production. A peasant whose land is further divided into small parcels at the birth of the next generation is unlikely to adopt new Western development techniques geared for a reasonable sized plot. Thus we note that while the Green Revolution has increased food production so that India now has about 20 million tons of food grain reserves, this benefit has come to the large farmers. Small farmers were driven to penury because they could not afford to invest in the new techniques. During the period of the Green Revolution in the sixties, the number of households below the poverty line increased from 38% in 1960 to 53% in 1968. It is just not appropriate to impose a model of development that is based on technology on to a society founded on assumptions of inequality. All aid, resources and inputs will flow into the existing structure and benefit those who benefit from the structure already.

It is unfortunate that much Christian thinking and practice coming from the West is based on the same assumptions as Western secular development that we have spelt out. This practice is reinforced where Christian agencies act through expatriates. Unfortunately my experience is that expatriates, even people filled with the Spirit, do not want to surrender their rights of leadership and are not encouraged by their agencies into taking new forms of responsibility without exercizing authoritarian roles. The practice is reinforced in the way that funds are administered. Where many separate Indian groups spring up to channel foreign funds, more gullible donors crop up to support them. In Andhra Pradesh alone, after the 1977 cyclone, at least 120 Church related agencies sprang into life to benefit from the ready supply of money available. Where Western agencies have priorities for the use of funds, or a date for completing the utilization of funds, these factors become dominant considerations in the decisions made on the ground. I set out how some of these factors operate in the following case studies.

Case Study 1
A village destroyed in a cyclone

After the worst cyclone this century on India's east coast, EFICOR provided immediate relief to some villages. The state allocated us a number of villages, including one where only one house remained standing. We realized that more was needed than food and clothes. We discussed with the villagers what they needed. They wanted houses. In dialogue with us they also saw the need for employment opportunities so that they could break out of bonded labour and so that the women could supplement their income. The people suggested trades that were appropriate for the area.

The large expenses involved meant we had to approach and consult foreign donors. They sent across representatives with experience in relief and rehabilitation in the Caribbean and the Americas. The Government advised us to provide cement concrete roofs for the new houses that would be constructed, and offered matching grants if those roofs were provided. These forms of houses would provide good protection and would require no maintenance. However, the foreign representatives insisted that we should provide the villagers with the sorts of houses that they had lived in before, made from wood, bamboo and palm leaves, but strengthened against future storms. We urged that the government's recommendations should be heeded. But to no avail. In the ensuing time taken over debate, the delay caused uncertainty among the villagers. In the end they sent our volunteers away as they felt that they were wasting their time.

Finally we settled for what we felt was second best. In one village we provided brick houses, but as a compromise put on tiled roofs instead of cement concrete ones. The tiles were made by the villagers, but the clay had to be imported from several miles away. However now, after eighteen months, these tiles are needing repair and replacement. It will be an expensive and difficult business to manufacture tiles that are needed.

In another 45 villages we followed the experts' advice and provided materials and skills for building traditional houses. Inevitably we lost heart somewhat as we had this policy forced on us. Had we not followed it we would have received no money at all. We had expected that our visitors would respect the views of their hosts who had worked in relief and development in their own country for a little time. After one year an assessor from the same agency who forced this policy on us came to review the programme. He discovered what we had feared. White ants and termites had eaten through the main supports of these traditional houses, and they were now useless. The funding programme of ¼ million pounds immediately halted. But the villagers were obviously left with the need to repair those houses each year, a process which costs about one month's salary each year. Unfortunately this mistake cannot be corrected, as to rebuild the village from scratch as we had the opportunity to do, would require another cyclone.

It saddened us to note that while the western agencies were sharp in pointing out to us our mistakes in some of our work, they were remarkably silent when mistakes occurred through the policy they forced on us. You may say that they have a right to make mistakes since their money is involved. I would respond by saying that a far more lasting impression would have been made by Christians on the Asiatic mind over the 300 years that westerners have been in India had they trusted and listened more to those of us who live here and understand the culture and the way people live and think. I think we all need to accept that we all are making mistakes as we learn, and we will continue to do so. Such acceptance is I think a mark of trust, respect and maturity in our relationships. To say 'I told you so' at every turn is not a positive way forward.

Case Study 2
A village hard hit by a flood

In the South Indian hills a freak period of rainfall caused heavy flooding, and swept away 68 houses in one village, drowning 12 people. A local Christian church, some local Christian business men and local Christian leaders got together and decided to do something. They approached EFICOR who immediately provided £550 for relief work.They then made plans for reconstructing the village. They decided on stone and concrete houses. A Christian contractor was employed and fine houses have been built. The occupants are paying 60 pence a head per house per month to defray some of the cost so that other people can be helped.

In this situation the money for the project came in very fast. There was no delay in getting the reconstruction going. I have to say that the reason was that there were two capable western people involved in the project whom the western agencies related to very positively; they asked for their opinion, and on receiving it sent the funds immediately.

I have no grumbles about this, especially as the project has gone well. However, this is not an ideal pattern. It should not be that in one situation money flows quickly to provide help simply because a resident foreigner is involved. Money in all situations should be entrusted to a Christian body, with clear responsibility, and some expertize in the field of relief and development. I am well aware that there are hundreds of cases where foreign agencies have been duped and money has been misspent. That is why I think there should be some national bodies with real responsibility who can vet projects periodically to check on wise stewardship. There is a real difference between such periodic vetting, and actually directing and deciding what shall be done from the start. This was not the case in this case-study I am happy to say. The contribution was positive, but it should not have been necessary.

Case Study 3
A training unit for community development organizers

As we have been involved in relief and development it has become clear that we have a great need for committed Christians from all parts of the country who not only understand that social action is part of the mission of the church, but who are also trained to engage in social action and motivate the church to be so involved.

We therefore proposed to set up a training unit to train people who grasped the clear biblical guidelines for Christian social action, and who would be long term workers in poor communities for development. These trainees would work in all parts of the country, they would equip many sections of the church in how to go forward in social action and in managing relief and development projects, and they could be called on in emergency situations to help channel and direct relief.

Our foreign partners saw the many ways in which such a programme would be valuable. They asked us a number of searching questions. Couldn't this training be found in already existing social training institutes in the country? We pointed out that our experience of the graduates of these institutions was that they were more concerned for advancement in their profession than for committed service to poor people. They were more interested in gaining fringe benefits, power and privileges than in living with and serving poor people. Such commitment required a deep Christian foundation. So our partners asked why we could not find such committed Christians and send them to these already existing institutes. We pointed out that we clearly felt that Christian social work needed to be taught from the point of of a clear biblical perspective. Our country has the largest population of Hindus in the world, and the second largest population of Moslems. You can't just take a secular approach to development and hope to win the Indian religious culture. You must take a specific Christian stance. Secular institutes would not train people in how to relate as Christians to poor Hindus and Moslems.

The partners noted that compared to the number of people we were proposing to take on each course, the costs per capita were very high. We pointed out that there were very few Christians as yet committed to this form of social involvement, that those who were educated enough to benefit from training in English were even fewer, and those who were prepared to rough it out in slums and villages were even fewer. If they were educated in English they could expect far easier jobs to come their way. We also pointed out that this was a pilot project and that mid-course corrections could be made as necessary.

So the plan we formulated and suggested was accepted. But the funding is still on an annual basis. This has some problems. It means that our permanent staff do not know from one year to the next if they will be retained next year. It also seems a pity to us to train and equip staff, and then be in danger of losing them if a more secure job comes their way or if the funds are withdrawn. Secondly it means that we are not in a position to respond to some of the invitations that come for seminars and courses during a year. We cannot overdraw on one year's budget to meet some requests, and then make up by underdrawing on the next.

One of the reasons of course why this project was able to go through with our plans intact was that we were under no time pressure to meet an emergency situation. There was time for discussion and explanation. In the emergency situation we described we knew that the longer we held out for what we thought best, the longer any substantial help was being denied to our countrymen. Unfortunately it is not possible to specify exact procedures and items for funding in advance in any emergency situation. For each situation is different. What is impossible is to import lessons and procedures from other cultures and other countries. You just have to trust the people of the land, and encourage their resources, dignity and responsibility by trusting their judgements. I actually think that people of the country can give a more objective assessment of needs in a relief situation than outsiders. Western minds are not as subtle as ours, and can be prey to manipulation to well-told stories and well-presented projects. My opinion is borne out by the existence of many examples where money has been poured into almost non-existent projects. Also, the overhigh profile of westerners in a situation can lead to misunderstandings. President Ford did Christian mission no service by telling the world that missionaries were the best sources of political information about a country. Every organization connected with the west in any way is automatically under suspicion, and every westerner who arrives to vet is suspected of having ulterior motives.

I am happy to say that at the present time, the same agency that has been involved with us in all our trials, is now assisting us very well in some new projects where we are making recommendations and finding very good co-operation. Hopefully we have all come some distance through the events we have experienced together.

Case Study 4
'How self-help is the best help' — a western oversimplification

Assistance from the West at crucial points is necessary. But there must be full consultation with development agencies in the area concerned.

In one instance gifts of jute and fishing tackle overnight enabled the weaker sections of some villages to become employed en masse. But the expatriates who initiated and supervized this did not realize that success in one area did not necessarily guarantee similar success in other area. Refugees in one area belonged to a community who considered begging outrageous. Therefore it was good stewardship to assist them with gifts of jute. But in another area, we have been struggling for two years to help disaster victims to regain independence by using the same methods of assistance, yet without success. This baffles the West. Proper consultation with Indian Christian development agencies can avoid such instances of bad stewardship.

Case Study 5
Traditional habits die hard

Some villages have for centuries been engaged only in the fishing industry, some only in leather foot-wear making and others only in bonded labour. Such traditions die hard. One authority told me that it took years to teach one group of villagers that it was more convenient to sit in a plastic chair that they could make than to sit on the floor. If Western churches in their aid insist that all castes can fish or learn to weave on looms simultaneously, they are giving an improper solution to changing traditional customs.

Case Study 6
Failure in community rehabilitation

A foreign church agency painted a dismal picture of a case of exploitation. Then through a loan the exploited people were weaned away from the clutches of unscrupulous middle men within a few months. A recent survey in the area show that in fact another floating population has replaced the first group in the middle-men's clutches. The first group has moved away into other parts of the city for better paid unskilled jobs. So a different process is now required to rehabilitate those who have taken their place in the slums.

Case Study 7
Problems due to direct action by foreign donors with individuals and groups in India

Western missionaries find it hard to avoid direct interaction with selected individuals and groups. They develop understandable affections for certain victims. When the missionaries return to their home land, those they have helped sometime later lose their testimony. They are tempted to build little empires, as the missionaries still collect donations for them.

A lace industry was financed by Western support for many years. It made a presentation to the Queen on her Silver Jubilee. On investigation it was found that for at least the last five years that agency did not exist. It had simply misused a steady supply of assistance for one individual's private benefit.

Case Study 8
Community survey unaccepted by donor agencies

One community surveyed its requirements for drinking water. It put up for acceptance a project for a number of wells. A Christian agency confirmed the need for the wells. But the donor agency's requirements meant that funds could be sent only for digging canals or strengthening embankments. So the money was not used for wells to benefit the villagers and the community. Instead it was used to help the Government do their normal job of digging canals and strengthening embankments.

Case Study 9
Unnecessary foreign interference in community development

a. Volunteers spent many months consoling disaster victims and came forward with several proposals. One was for cement housing. Foreign experts later arrived with expertize gained in Nicaragua and Guatemala. They preferred to fund wood and bamboo houses strengthened against high winds. After one year over forty villages were reconstructed using strengthened wood and bamboo houses. But it was found that the local termites and white ants devoured wood more voraciously than those found in Nicaragua. All the 42 villages now need extensive, expensive repair work on the houses. The disaster experts had not realized this aspect of the problem.

b. A local students' survey team advocated that two villages be reconstructed with cement concrete houses. The people had been suffering under bonded labour for generations and the provision of houses was a definite improvement for them. The houses proved cool and comfortable. They provided a work site for the women and children and have helped break the yoke of bonded labour. Unfortunately the donor agency has stopped their funding without warning and the people are being forced back to bonded (slave) labour.

c. A church funding agency required that its grants be used by a certain date line to suit its own audit requirements. The work was rushed through and contractors and middle-men dissipated a lot of money. The opportunity for villagers to become self-reliant was lost. However, the Western agency was very pleased and commended the speed and efficiency of the work.

Case Study 10
Pitfalls of specifications and time limits

a. It was decided that low-lying areas which had been inundated by a tidal wave should be desalinated. But a foreign agency stipulated that disaster relief should be used for seedlings and saplings. The soil could not be desalinated within the time limit set by the agency for the completion of the planting of seedlings and saplings.

b. One agency insisted on giving aid only to children and another on giving aid only to the aged. Neither specification could be properly met within the time limit given, so many children who were not orphans were inducted into the programme and a number of able-bodied people got away with several benefits. The people who suffered were the poorest for whom the aid was designated.

Case Study 11
Government credit facilities untapped

a. The Government and the Banks give credit facilities for buffaloes and cows or loans for projects like providing cycle rickshaws. A relief agency stands security that the loan is repaid regularly. But some donors think that the right action in a disaster is to replace livestock immediately and so unnecessarily duplicate existing resources.

b. Large Western Christian farming agencies insist on saturating a disaster area with money for seedlings and fertilizers. The disaster victims are not in immediate need of these. As a result the Government experts who are mandated to provide these can sit idle and do nothing.

Case Study 12
Misuse of development money

a. A European source provided fishing equipment for some villages on the sea coast. But only some of the villagers were fishermen by trade. So only 15% of the valuable nylon nets were used for fishing. The rest were purchased in bulk by wealthy contractors for the prawn trawler industry which is controlled by rich men.

b. Seven million tiles were made for one particular village at the instigation of foreign experts. Clay soil was brought from several miles away so that about 200 people could learn the skill of making tiles. But now that they can make tiles, there is no means for bringing the clay into the sandy areas were they live. They cannot leave their houses to move to where the clay soil is found. As a result there is a real dilemma about whether and how they can follow up these newly acquired skills. A roof of local materials, including cement, might have been an adequate substitute for that offered by foreign technology. As it was, there was no way that the disaster victims could object to the foreign advice that was imposed on them.

Case Study 13
Poor investigations of fraternal organizations

Quite a number of privately registered family societies sprang up and presented sizeable budgets for funding to fraternal churches in the West. The registered society turned out to be members and relatives of one family. So all the property is legally theirs. Nothing can be done to use the funds to alleviate the distress of the poor victims from whom they were sent, or to recover the funds.

Summary of Apparent Contradictions and Mistakes

a. For technical and managerial reasons, foreign countries expect to export theologies or assumptions that are more familiar and successful at home.
b. There is a failure to understand and respect historical structures of hindu caste systems, traditional values and bonded labour.
c. Western agencies sometimes fail to provide an immediate and timely response to Third World disasters. They sometimes extend assistance only on receipt of confirmation by Western disaster experts.
d. The ability of Western expatriates to tackle any Eastern problem is oversimplified.
e. Expertize gained in other disaster areas is not necessarily relevant in other Third World countries.
f. So-called success is reinforced by sending more expatriates.
g. Equality is needed in the decision-making process between donor and national agencies.
h. Poor stewardship and losses occur when well-meaning missionaries help selected individuals who build up private empires on little known church groups who later prove to be spurious and registered societies consisting of one set of family members.
i. Surveys and assessments of priorities by the local communities are not respected while sometimes credit facilities available through the government or banks are duplicated through insufficient information and investigation.
j. The pressure to utilize funds to suit the date line requirements of Western auditors rushes projects and leads to improper selection of beneficiaries.
k. Dislocation is caused when ongoing development projects are suddenly defunded without adequate warning.

The ultimate goal in mission is the final revelation of the Kingdom of God — the total transformation and development of history by Jesus Christ at his return. But before the end of the world, God's Kingdom is present in this world forming a new community. This community experiences and expresses forgiveness of sins. It issues the call of the kingdom of God to repentance, faith, sharing and caring. The lifestyle of the kingdom is based on love. The practical expression of this love is justice, mercy, truth and servanthood in the socio-political areas.

The mission of the church has its source and model in the mission of Jesus. 'As the Father has sent me, so send I you' (John 20:21). The church is to incarnate the gospel of Christ in word and deed so that men and women become faithful disciples of Christ.

Development is therefore the work of God in history. God's purpose in the life, death and resurrection of Jesus was to bring life more abundant, to enable persons to become truly human. As we share God's purpose we commit ourselves to serve all men for their true development, so that they can experience abundant life.

Therefore any relationship between First and Third World Churches should express:

a. A partnership of equal dignity and equality in common fellowship in Jesus Christ.

b. A common dependence on God to seek his vision in discovering the real needs of a situaiton and how to meet them.

c. A common motivation in discipleship to Jesus Christ who identified himself with the poor, hungry, homeless and helpless. These are the people who now inhabit the Third World.

d. A common role of servanthood to all.

Appendix

Co-ordinator

Ronald J. Sider
Associate Professor of Theology
Eastern Baptist Theological Seminary
Philadelphia, PA, U.S.A.

Participants

Miriam Adeney
Anthropologist/Writer
U.S.A.

John F. Alexander, Director
Jubilee Fund
U.S.A.

Peter Batchelor
Consultant, RURCON
England

Ruth Batchelor
Consultant, RURCON
England

Wayne Bragg, Director
HNGR Program
Wheaton College
U.S.A.

Robert M. Cuthbert, Gen. Secretary
Caribbean Conference of Churches
Kingston
Jamaica

Joshua Daimoi
Bible Society of Papua New Guinea
Papua, New Guinea

Donald Dayton
Assoc. Professor of Historical
  Theology
Northern Baptist Theological
  Seminary
U.S.A.

Edward R. Dayton, Director
Evangelism & Research Division
World Vision International
U.S.A.

Jorgen Glenthoj
Free Faculty of Theology
Denmark

Paul Hampsch, Assistant Director
Long Range Development
Youth With a Mission
U.S.A.

Simon A. Ibrahim, Gen. Secretary
Evangelical Churches of West
  Africa
Nigeria

Neuza Itioka, Second V. President
Alianca Biblical Universitaria
Brazil

Israel Katoke
Regional Advisor for Culture in
   Africa
UNESCO
Senegal

Graham Kerr, Director
Long Range Development
Youth With a Mission
U.S.A.

Andrew Kirk
England

Manfred W. Kohl, Director
World Vision
Germany

Vishal Mangalwadi, Secretary
Assoc. for Comprehensive Rural
   Assistance
Christian Hospital
India

Chris Marantika
Indonesia

Col. Ron Mathews, Director
EFICOR
India

Bruce McConchie, Director
TEAR Fund (NZ)
New Zealand

Bruce J. Nicholls, Exec. Secretary
WEF Theological Commission
India

Robin Nicoll
Planning & Evaluation Adviser
TEAR Fund (UK)
England

Terry Norr, Asst. to the President
Mission Aviation Fellowship
U.S.A.

Shadrack W. Opoti, Director
Christian Rural Service
Kenya

Rene Padilla, Editor
Ediciones Certeza, I.F.E.S.
Argentina

Gustavo A. Parajon, Director
PROVADENIC
Nicaragua

D. John Richard, Exec. Director
Evangelical Fellowship of India
India

John F. Robinson
Director of Program Development
MAP International
U.S.A.

Vinay Samuel
Pastor, Theologian
India

Paul G. Schrotenboer
Gen. Secretary
Reformed Ecumenical Synod
U.S.A.

Waldron Scott, General Secretary
World Evangelical Fellowship
U.S.A.

Ronald J. Sider, President
Evangelicals for Social Action
U.S.A.

Maurice Sinclair
Asst. Gen. Secretary
South American Missionary Society
England

Tom Sine
Co-ordinator for Research Planning
   & Education
World Concern/Crista International
U.S.A.

Kevin Smith, Assistant Director
TEAR Fund (Australia)
Australia

Chris Sugden
EFICOR Educational and Training
   Unit
India

Jun Vencer, Executive Director
Philippine Council of Evangelical
   Churches
Philippines

Roger Walker
Director of Relief and Development
World Vision of Australia
Australia

Robert L. Youngblood
Admin. Assistant
WEF Theological Commission
U.S.A.

Chris Wigglesworth
Lecturer in Practical Theology
Aberdeen University
Scotland

Notes

INTRODUCTION (pages 9-12)

1. *Newsweek*, Feb. 18, 1980, p.63
2. *The Global Report to the President: Entering the Twenty-First Century,* Vol. I (Washington: U.S. Government Printing Office, 1980), p.1.
3 *North-South: A Programme for Survival* (Report of the Independent Commission on International Development Issues; London: Pan Books Ltd., 1980), p.8,
4. Initial planning occurred in early Sept. 1978 at the impetus of Bruce Nicholls, Executive Secretary of the Theological Commission of the WEF whose conversations with persons in various parts of the world suggested the need for an evangelical study on the nature of development from a biblical perspective. With the help of World Relief Commission, Wayne Bragg, Bruce Nicholls, John Robinson, Vinay Samuel and Ronald J. Sider attended this planning session. The Unit on Ethics and Society then invited representatives of development agencies, theologians and development practitioners to come together in April, 1979 to determine the need for an international consultation. With the financial assistance of World Relief Commission and Tear Fund (UK), 12 people met at Ventnor, N.J. on April 4, 1979. It was decided to proceed, basic direction was determined, and a Steering Committee composed of Wayne Bragg, John Robinson, Vinay Samuel, Ronald J. Sider, Tom Sine, and Jun Vencer was named to complete the arrangements.
5. The members of the Steering Committee are: Arthur Beals, World Concern; David Chambers, World Relief Commission; Wade Coggins, EFMA; Edward R. Dayton, World Vision; Jorgen Glenthoj, Free Faculty of Theology, Borum, Denmark; Simon Ibrahim, Evangelical Churches of West Africa; Israel Katoke, UNESCO; Andrew Kirk, Pastor, England; Ron Mathews, Evangelical Fellowship of India Committee on Relief; Rene Padilla, IFES; Gustavo Parajon, PROVADENIC; Vinay Samuel, Pastor/Theologian, India; Ronald J. Sider, Eastern Baptist Theological Seminary; Kevin Smith, Tear Fund (Australia); Jun Vencer, Philippine Council of Evangelical Churches; Siegfried Wiesinger, Christoffelblinden mission.
6. Paper I "What is Development? A Definition"; Paper II "A Biblical Approach to Development"; Paper III "Development, Freedom and Justice"; Paper IV "Development and the Church"; Paper V "Development and Eschatology"; Paper VI "Culture and Development".

CHAPTER TWO (pages 19-42)

1. From a collection of definitions gathered by Donald Miller of MAP International.
2. The material on Augustine and the Reformation is from *"Through a Glass Darkly: A History of the Church's Vision of the Poor and Poverty"* by Carter H. Lindberg of the Institute for Ecumenical Research, Strasbourg, an unpublished lecture. November 1979.
3. Lindberg op. cit. p.6.
4. Lindberg op. cit. pp.10-11.
5. On the call for moratorium see the debate in *International Review of Mission* April 1975, and "The Call to Moratorium" Michael Cassidy, Churchman, Oct-Dec 1976. On expansion, by-passing the national church if necessary, see *"Do we really want a national church?"* Editorial in MARC Newsletter November 1979 p.6.
6. Material available from theologians of liberation is rapidly expanding. Four introductory surveys available in English are:

   Alberto Fierro *The Militant Gospel* (SCM 1977)
   Andrew Kirk *Liberation Theology An Evangelical View from the Third World* (Marshall Morgan and Scott 1979)
   Theology Encounters Revolution (IVP 1980)
   Derek Winter *Hope in Captivity* (Epworth Press 1977)

   Contributors to the debate in English from Latin America include the following:

   Ruben Alves *A Theology of Human Hope* (World Publishing Co. 1969. Abbey Press 1972)
   Tomorrow's Child (SCM 1972)
   Hugo Assmann *Theology for a Nomad Church* (Orbis Books 1976) published as *Practical Theology of Liberation* (Search Press 1975)
   Jose Miguez Bonino *Doing Theology in a Revolutionary Situation* (Fortress Press 1975) published as *Revolutionary Theology Comes of Age* (SPCK 1975)
   Christians and Marxists: The Mutual Challenge to Revolution (Hodder and Stoughton 1976)
   Helder Camara *Church and Colonialism* (Sheed and Ward 1969)
   The Desert is Fertile (Sheed and Ward 1974)
   Race against Time (Sheed and Ward)
   Revolution Through Peace (Harper Colophon Books 1971)
   The Spiral of Violence (Sheed and Ward 1971)
   Emilio Castro *Amidst Revolution* (Christian Journals Ltd. 1975)
   Orlando Costas *The Church and Its Mission: A Shattering Critique from the Third World* (Tyndale House Publishers 1974)
   Samuel Escobar "Evangelization and Man's Search for Freedom, Justice and Fulfilment" in J. D. Douglas, ed. *Let the Earth Hear His Voice* (Minneapolis 1975)
   "The Kingdom of God, Eschatology, and Social and Political Ethics in Latin America" in *Bulletin of the Latin American Theological Fraternity* 1975 No. 1.

"The Formation of the People of God in the Large Cities" in the
Bulletin of the LATF 1979 No. 2.

Paulo Freire *Cultural Action for Freedom* (Penguin 1972)
Pedagogy of the Oppressed (Penguin 1972)
Education, Liberation and the Church Study Encounter 1973 Vol IX
No. 1

John Gerassi (ed) *The Revolutionary Priest: The Complete Writings and
Message of Camilo Torres* (Jonathan Cape 1971)

Gustavo Guttierez *A Theology of Liberation* (SCM 1974)

Jose Porfirio Miranda *Marx and the Bible* (SCM 1977)

Rene Padilla "Evangelism and the World" in J. D. Douglas ed, *Let the
Earth Hear His Voice* (Minneapolis 1975)

Rene Padilla "The Kingdom of God and the Church" in *Bulletin of the
LATF* 1976 Nos. 1, 2

"Partnership in Mission' in *Bulletin of the LATF* July 1978, and in
Evangelical Review of Theology October 1979 p.225

"Liberation Theology" in *Share the Word* (Ark Publishing (SU) 1979)
p.76

Jose Maria Gonzalez-Ruiz *The New Creation — Marxist or Christian*
(Orbis 1976)

Julio de Santa Ana *Good News to the Poor: The Challenge of the Poor in
the History of the Church* (Geneva 1977 Madras 1978)

Juan Luis Segundo *Theology for the Artisans of a New Humanity* (Orbis
1973-4)
Vol I The Community called Church
Vol II Grace and the Human Condition
Vol III Our Idea of God
Vol IV The Sacraments Today
Vol V Evolution and Guilt
The Liberation of Theology (Orbis 1976)

7. Members of the Fraternity include Samuel Escobar, Rene Padilla, Peter
Savage, Orlando Costas, Pablo Perez, and, until his return to England,
Andrew Kirk. The LATF Bulletin is available from The Co-Ordinator,
Apartado D 67, Cuernavaca, Morelos, Mexico.

8. From "Theology Implications of Radical Discipleship" in J. D. Douglas
ed. *Let the Earth Hear His Voice* (Minneapolis 1975), pp.1294-6; *International Review of Mission* October 1974 pp.574-6.

9. See especially Rene Padilla "The Kingdom of God and the Church" *Bulletin of the LATF* 1976 1, 2.

10. Michael Eastman "Liberation Theology: A Response" in *Share the Word*
(Ark Publishing (SU) 1979) p.87.

11. *The First Assembly of the World Council of Churches, the Official
Report* edited by W. A. Visser 'T Hooft SCM 1949 Report on Section III
— The Church and the Disorder of Society pp.74-82.

12. "The Meaning of Man in the Debate Between Christianity and Marxism"
in *Themelios* Spring and Summer 1976.

13. For example, while India's GNP per capita is 150 dollars, the lowest in
Middle and South America are Honduras and Bolivia with 390 dollars.

Argentina, Chile and Brazil are all over 1000 dollars. Source: Population Reference Bureau Washington.

14. "From Israel to Asia: A Theological Leap" by Choan-Seng Song in *Mission Trends No. 3 Third World Theologies* edited by Anderson and Stransky (Paulist/Eerdmans 1976) pp.219-220.

15. From a summary of "New Frontiers of Theology in Asia: Ten Theological Theses" by Choan-Seng Song reproduced in *Partnerscan* Vol IV, No. 4 August 1979 pp.9-14 from *Ching Feng*. Song is associate director of the Faith and Order Commission of the World Council of Churches.

16. "From Israel to Asia: A Theological Leap" op. cit. pp.217-8.

17. M. M. Thomas occupies a prominent position among Indian theologians. His book *Salvation and Humanization* CLS Madras 1971 set forth his idea of "a Christ-centred secular fellowship outside the Church". Thomas and Newbigin discuss this in "Salvation and Humanization" in *Mission Trends No. 1,* edited by Anderson and Stransky (Paulist/Eerdmans 1974) pp.217f. See also Thomas's books *Man and the Universe of Faiths* CLS Madras 1975 and *The Secular Ideologies of India and the Secular Meaning of Christ* CLS Madras 1976 for his thesis of Christianity's humanizing effect.

18. Sebastian Kappen is a Roman Catholic theologian of liberation who analyzes Indian culture as a culture of oppression, which always rejects or absorbs any form of protest against its religiously sanctioned injustices. His work *Jesus and Freedom* was published by Orbis in 1977. His monthly leaflets *Anawim* and *Socialist Perspectives* develop his thinking.

19. For these ideas see the following papers by Samuel and Sugden: "Mission in the Eighties — An Asian Perspective" *Occasional Bulletin of Missionary Research* April 1980; "Identifying Indian Evangelical Theology" in *TRACI Journal* April 1979; "What does it mean to confess Jesus as Lord in India Today?" a paper presented to the faculty of United Theological College, Bangalore.

20. "The Economic Gospel of Jesus" by Vishal Mangalwadi in *TRACI Journal* April 1979 and *Evangelical Review of Theology* October 1979 p.259.

21. For Nyerere's thought see *Freedom and Socialism* CUP 1968, *Man and Development*, "The Economic Challenge: Dialogue or Confrontation" in the *Journal of the Royal Commonwealth Society* 1976, and "The development of peoples and the meaning of service" *Mission Trends* No. 1 edited by Anderson and Stransky (Paulist/Eerdmans 1974).

22. From *Man and Development* by Julius Nyerere.

23. From "Is Poverty the Real Problem?" address by Julius Nyerere to the Maryknoll Sisters' General Chapter New York 1970, extracts published by Indian Social Institute, Bangalore p.3.

24. John Mbiti surveys *The South African Theology of Liberation: Appreciation and Evaluation* in *A Vision for Man* edited by Samuel Amirtham (CLS Madras 1978) pp.348ff. Mbiti bases his work on the book *Black Theology: The South African Voice* (American title: *The Challenge of Black Theology in South Africa*) edited by Basil Moore (C. Hurst and Co. London 1973). Butheleze's quote is on p.100 of the Moore volume, and p.352 of Mbiti's essay.

25. Mpynize's quote is on p.139 of the Moore volume, p.355 of Mbiti's essay.
26. Byang Kato "Black Theology and African Theology" in *Evangelical Review of Theology* October 1977 pp.36-37.
27. Kato op. cit. p.38.
28. Kato op. cit. p.38-9.
29. Kato op. cit. p.45.
30. Tite Tienou "Christianity and African Culture: A Review" in *Evangelical Review of Theology* October 1979 p.205.
31. John S. Mbiti "Christianity and African Culture" in *Evangelical Review of Theology* October 1979 pp.183, 187, 195.
32. Tienou op. cit. p.203.
33. Mbiti "Theological Impotence and the Universality of the Church" in *Mission Trends No. 3 Third World Theologies* edited by Anderson and Stransky (Paulist/Eerdmans 1976) p.17.
34. Choan-Seng Song "New Frontiers of Theology in Asia: Ten Theological Theses" Abstract in *Partnerscan* Vol IV No. 4 August 1979 op. cit. pp.9-10.
35. Klaus Nurnberger ed. *Affluence, Poverty and the Word of God* (Lutheran Publishing House Durban 1978).
36. Klaus Nurnberger "The Development Debate: Ideological Evasion and Christian Obedience" in *Affluence, Poverty and the Word of God* op. cit. p.223.
37. Nurnberger op. cit. p.224.
38. Nurnberger op. cit. p.230.
39. Adam Smith *An Inquiry into the Nature and Causes of the Wealth of Nations* 1776 Book V. Ch. II.
40. See for example Alan Storkey *A Christian Social Perspective* (IVP 1979) ch. 13; A. B. Cramp *Notes Towards a Christian Critique of Secular Economic Theory* Institute of Christian Studies 1975; Donald Hay *A Christian Critique of Capitalism* (Grove Books 1975); E. F. Schumacher *Small is Beautiful* (Sphere 1974); Philip Wogaman *The Great Economic Debate* (SCM and Westminster Press 1977); William Temple *Christianity and Social Order* (repub. SPCK 1976).
41. John Bennett *Christian Values and Economic Life* (Harper 1954 and 1970) p.6.
42. F. Ernest Johnson *The Church and Society* (Abingdon Press New York 1935) pp.221f quoted in Bennett op. cit. p.7.
43. Bennett op. cit. pp.4 and 6.
44. See William Davies *It's No Sin to be Rich* for a spirited apologia for these men.
45. See for example Sir Frederick Catherwood *A Better Way* (IVP 1975) for a representative of this position.
46. For Frank's exposition of this thesis see his *Capitalism and Underdevelopment in Latin America* (Penguin 1971).
47. See the authors mentioned in note 40, and the survey of recent writing on Capitalism and Socialism in Christian Mission and The Utopian Dream, special issue of *SCAN* Partnership in Mission Spring 1978.
48. Stephen Mott "A Political Philosophy for Elephants in the Chicken

Yard" *Vanguard* March-April 1977, abstracted in *SCAN* Spring 1978 pp.13-14.

CHAPTER THREE (pages 45-67)

1. See Vinay Samuel and Chris Sugden "What Does It Mean to Confess Jesus as Lord in India Today?" unpublished paper; *In Search of a Theology of Development* (Sodepax 1970) p.51 summarized by Charles Elliott in *The Development Debate* (SCM 1971).
2. See for example the work of Robert McAfee Brown and Richard Shaull. A collection of these writers is gathered in *Mission Trends No. 4* North American and European Perspectives on Liberation Edited by Anderson and Stransky (Paulist/Eerdmans 1979).
3. Among Martin Luther King's writings we particularly note *Chaos or Community* (Hodder and Stoughton 1968), "Letter from Birmingham Jail" in *On Being Responsible* ed. J. M. Gustafson and J. T. Laney p.256 (SCM 1969), *The Trumpet of Conscience* (Hodder and Stoughton 1968), *Strength to Love* (Fontana 1974).

   James H. Cone's major works are *A Black Theology of Liberation* (Lippincott Philadelphia 1970), *Black Theology and Black Power* (Seabury New York 1969), *God of the Oppressed* (Seabury New York 1975). Jan Luis Segundo gives a very helpful guide to James Cone's thought in *Liberation of Theology* (Orbis 1976) pp.25-34. He describes his method as a fine example of taking the hermeneutical circle through its four stages: i) a commitment to the poor ii) a theory to explain their poverty iii) deciding the major questions to ask the biblical text iv) asking those questions of the text. Cone finds the basis of exploitation not in economic differences which form different classes, but in the racial difference which is rooted far more deeply in human psychology. In his treatment of the biblical material he asks whether "the love of God itself can be properly understood without focussing equally on the biblical view of God's righteousness". Biblical Theology of Liberation p.79-80.
4. John Yoder *The Politics of Jesus* (Eerdmans 1972).
5. See Jim Wallis *Agenda for Biblical People* (Harper 1976).
6. For example, the Mayflower Centre in Canning Town under the leadership of David Sheppard for many years, St. George's Crypt, Leeds, for homeless men, the Cambridge University Mission in Bermondsey, the Oxford-Kilburn Club in London and Shaftesbury House in Everton had all been involved in ministries of social concern as evangelical foundations for a number of years.
7. (Falcon 1975).
8. (Inter Varsity USA 1977, Hodder UK 1978).
9. Lausanne Covenant Paragraph 5 on Christian Social Responsibility.
10. John Stott *Christian Mission in the Modern World* op. cit. p.30. For a full discussion of this view see John Gladwin "Politics, Providence and the Kingdom" *Churchman* January 1977 pp.47-57.
11. See for an example of this view of development Edward R. Dayton *Some Introductory Thoughts on Evangelization and Development* Pasadena Consultation Paper 1977.
12. Amidst the growing literature on the kingdom of God as a central theme in the Bible and for Christian mission we cite the following:

John Bright *The Kingdom of God* (Abingdon 1953)

J. D. Douglas ed. *Let the Earth Hear His Voice* (Minneapolis 1975) papers by Samuel Escobar "Evangelization and Man's Search for Freedom, Justice and Fulfilment", Andrew Kirk "The Kingdom of God and the Church in Contemporary Protestantism and Roman Catholicism", Rene Padilla "Evangelism and the World"

Samuel Escobar "The Kingdom of God, Eschatology and Social and Political Ethics in Latin America' in *Bulletin of the Latin American Theological Fraternity* 1975 Vol. 1

International Review of Mission Vol. LXVIII No. 270 April 1979 "Your Kingdom Come'

Joachim Jeremias *The Sermon on the Mount* (Fortress)

Al Krass *Five Lanterns at Sundown* (Eerdmans 1978)

G. E. Ladd *The Presence of the Future* (Eerdmans 1974)
Theology of the New Testament (Eerdmans 1974)
I Believe in the Resurrection of Jesus (Hodder 1975)

I. Howard Marshall "Preaching the Kingdom of God" in *Expository Times* October 1977 pp.13-16

Jose Miguez-Bonino "Kingdom of God, Utopia, and Historical Engagement" in *Doing Theology in a Revolutionary Situation* (Fortress 1974) pp.131-53

Rene Padilla "The Kingdom of God and the Church" *Bulletin of the LATF* 1976 Nos. 1, 2

Wolfhart Pannenberg *Theology and the Kingdom of God* (Westminster 1969)

Ray C. Petry *Christian Eschatology and Social Thought* (Abingdon 1956)

Christopher Sugden "The Kingdom and the Kingdoms" in *Third Way* Vol 1, No. 13 (June 30, 1977), and Vol 1, No. 14 (July 14, 1977)
Social Gospel or No Gospel (Grove Books 1975)

John Yoder *The Politics of Jesus* (Eerdmans 1972).

13. See further the discussion by Rene Padilla in "Evangelism and the World" in *Let the Earth Hear His Voice* ed. J. D. Douglas (Minneapolis 1975).

14. See John 1:3, 1 Cor 8:6, Col. 1:19-20.

15. See Vinay Samuel *Theological Reflection on Development in India* paper presented to the All-India Conference on Evangelical Social Action Madras 1979.

16. See Amos's judgment on the surrounding nations in Amos 1 and 2, and Jonah's preaching to Nineveh.

17. Amos 9:7.

18. Luke 19:42.

19. John 3:19.

20. John 1:4-5.

21. John 3:17-21.

22. Rom. 2:4.

23. John 16:4-11.

24. 1 Tim 2:1-4.

25. See David Clines "The Image of God in Man" *Tyndale Bulletin* No. 19, 1968.

26. For a concise summary of the discussion see Ron Sider *Evangelism Salvation and Social Justice* (Grove Books 1976) with response by John Stott.
27. See Col. 2:13-15, Eph. 1:20-23.
28. See for example T. W. Manson in *Peake's Commentary* on Romans 8.
29. John F. Robinson *Toward Understanding Development in Biblical Perspective* Pasadena Consultation Paper 1977 pp.4-5.
30. Charles Kraft *Christianity in Culture* (Orbis 1979) pp.53-57 summarized by David Lim in *Cultural Sensitivity in Hermeneutics* unpublished paper p.4.
31. J. Philip Wogaman *The Great Economic Debate* (SCM/Fortress 1977) p.10.
32. See Donald Hay *A Christian Critique of Capitalism* op. cit. and Wogaman op. cit.
33. Reported in *SCAN* spring 1978 op. cit. p.2.
34. Carter Lindberg op. cit. note 2 p.16.
35. Harvie Conn "The Mission of the Church" in *Evangelicals and Liberation* edited by Carl E. Armerding (Presbyterian and Reformed Publishing 1977) pp.63-4.
36. Reported in Editorial of *Christian Century* Feb. 28 1979.
37. See Robin Boyd *India and the Latin Captivity of the Church* Cambridge 1974.
38. Among western evangelicals who have expressed a critical assessment of Liberation Theology see the essays by Stephen Mott and Harvie Conn in *Evangelicals and Liberation* op. cit. On an ecumenical level see the surveys and summaries of Brian Wren *Education for Justice* (SCM 1977); Richard N. Dickinson *To Set at Liberty the Oppressed*(WCC 1975); the collection of essays in *In Search of a Theology of Development* (Sodepax 1970); and Charles Elliott *The Development Debate* (SCM 1971).
39. "What do you think of the Madras Declaration?" *AIM Magazine* New Delhi December 1979.
40. "World Poverty and Christian Responsibility" Michael Alison M.P. *Christian Graduate* UCCF Leicester December 1979.
41. See the debate in *Evangelism, Salvation, and Social Justice* (Grove Books 1977) between Ron Sider and John Stott.
42. See the review by Martin Goldsmith of Andrew Kirk *Liberation Theology — An Evangelical View from the Third World* (Marshall Morgan and Scott 1979) in *Third Way* February 1980 p.30. "And yet some critics may feel that this book lacks an adequate emphasis on the atonement, the resurrection and the Holy Spirit — the author assumes these fundamental truths, implies and even mentions them but should they be primary in the argument?"
43. The phrase is John Stott's.
44. For further discussion see "Partnership: Key to Church Credibility in the Third World" by Vinay Samuel and Chuck Corwin *Evangelical Missions Quarterly* April 1979 and *Evangelical Review of Theology* April 1980.
45. For a complete bibliography on theology of development up to 1970 consult *Towards a Theology of Development* An Annotated Bibliography compiled by G. Bauer (Sodepax 1970).

CHAPTER FOUR (pages 71-86)

1. Walberg Buhlmann, *The Coming of the Third Church* (New York: Orbis Books, 1977) p.42.
2. David Morawetz, *Twenty-Five Years of Economic Development* (Washington, D.C., World Bank, 1977) p.7.
3. John Sommers, *Beyond Charity: U.S. Voluntary Aid for a Changing Third World* (Washington D.C., Overseas Development Council, 1977) p.3.
4. Larry Collins and Dominique LaPierre, *Freedom at Midnight* (New York: Simon Schuster, 1975).
5. Jeremy Rifkin and Ted Howard, *The Emerging Order: God in the Age of Scarcity* (New York: G. P. Putnam's Sons, 1979) p.25.
6. Rifkin op. cit. p.33.
7. Rifkin op. cit. p.34.
8. Martin McLaughlin, *The United States and World Development: Agenda 1979* (New York: Praeger Publishing, 1979) p.25.
9. "Technology and Population", United States Office of Technology Assessment, 21 August 1978, p.2.
10. Cees Hamelink, *The Corporate Village: The Role of Transnational Corporations in International Communication* (Rome: IDCC Europe Dossier Four, 1977) p.11.
11. Richard J. Barnet, "Multinationals and Development" M. E. Jegen and C. K. Wilber, editors, *Growth with Equity: Strategies for Meeting Human Needs* (New York: Paulist Press, 1979) p.149.
12. Beverley Keene "Export-cropping in Central America" (Background Paper No. 43, Bread for the World, New York, January 1980).
13. S. Enzer, R. Drobnick and S. Alter, "World Food Prospects: The Next Twenty Years", *The Futurist*, 1978, p.288.
14. Jan Tinberger (Ed.) *Rio: Reshaping the Internal Economic Order* (New York: E. P. Dutton and Company, Inc., 1976) p.31.
15. "Hemisphere Trends", *Americas*, January 1979, p.17.
16. R. L. Sivard, "World Military and Social Expenditures" (Background Paper No. 21, Bread for the World, February 1978).

Index